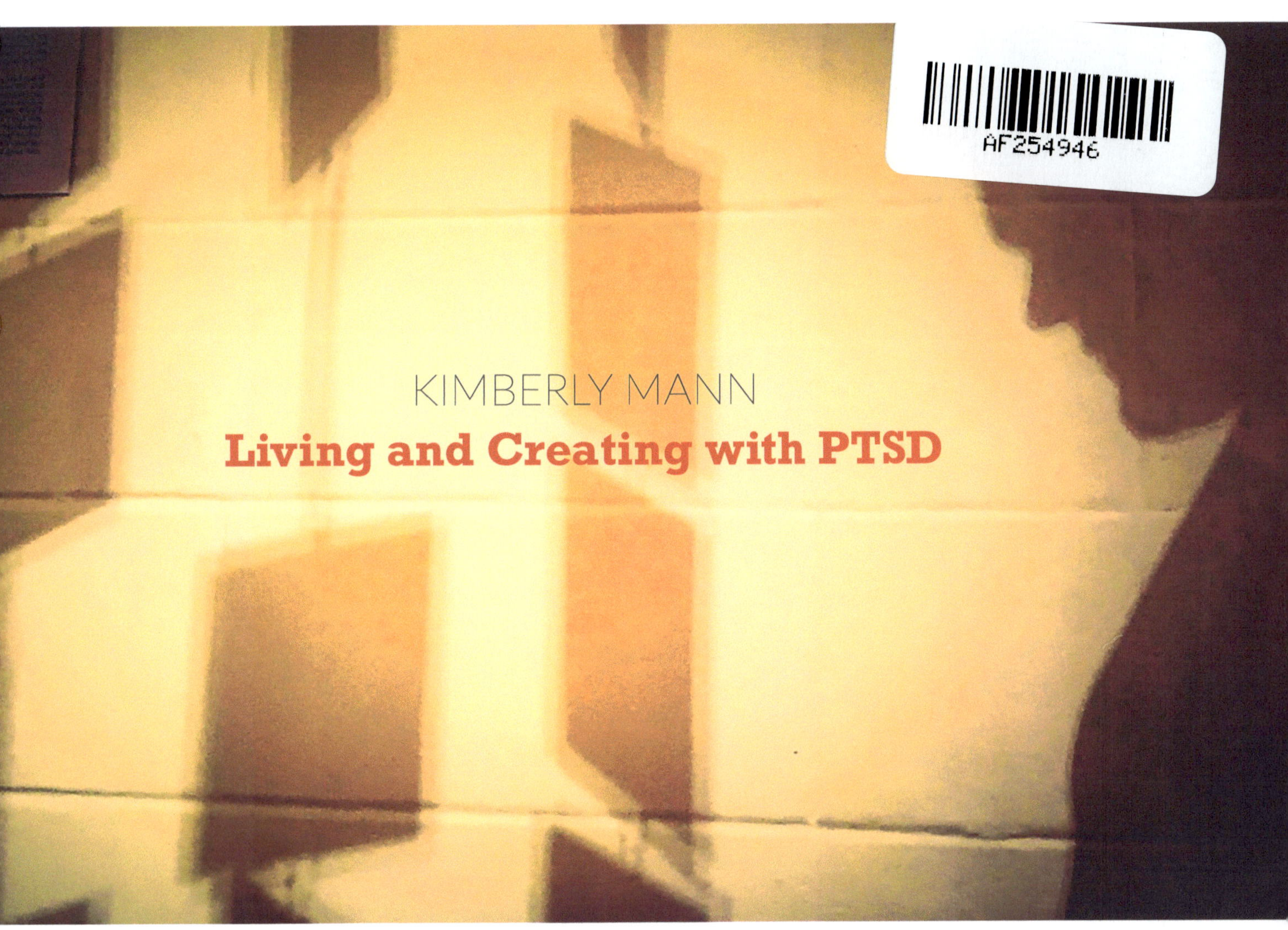
KIMBERLY MANN
Living and Creating with PTSD
An Artist's Expression of Surviving Post-Traumatic Stress Disorder

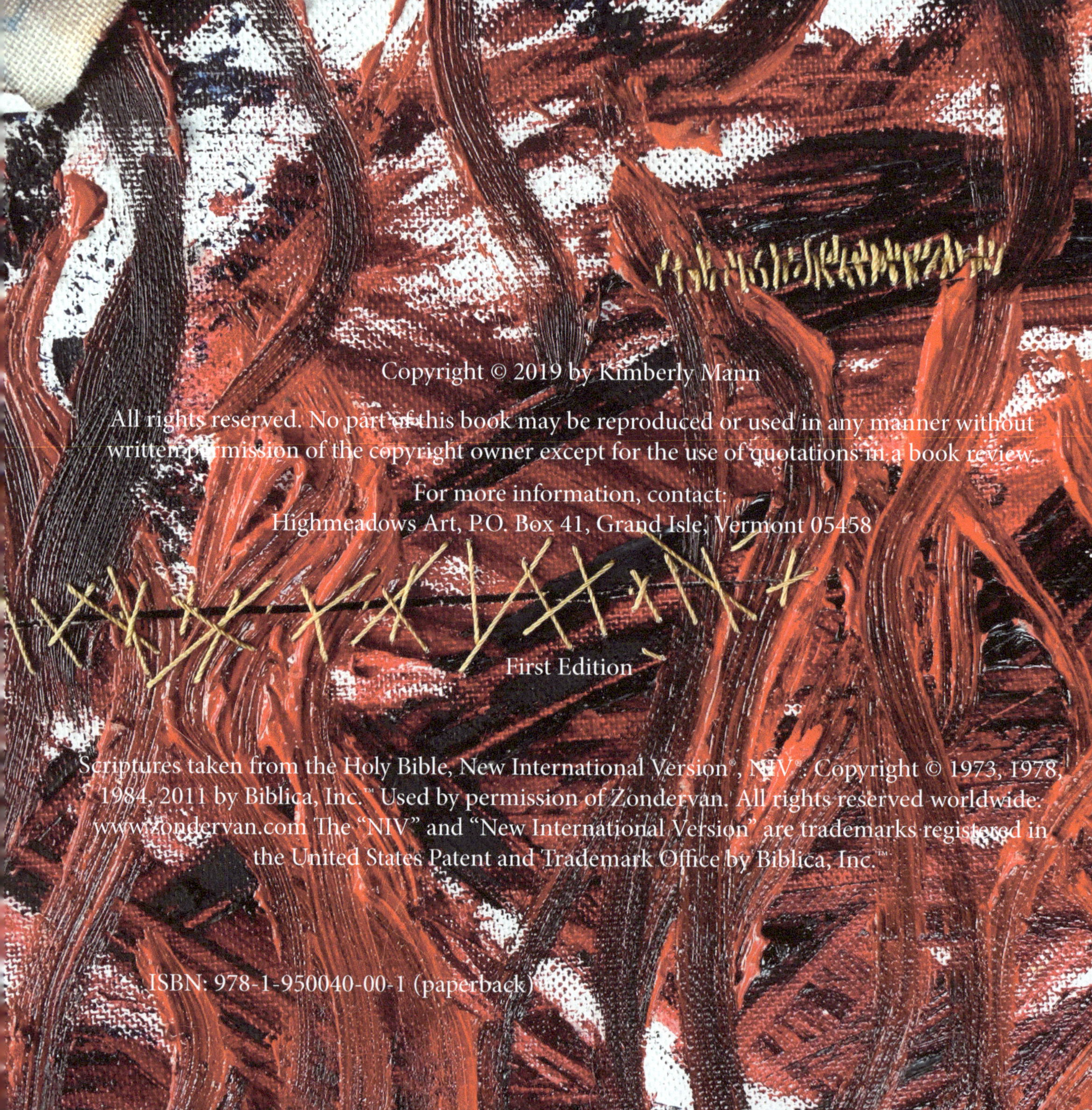

For more information, contact:
Highmeadows Art, P.O. Box 41, Grand Isle, Vermont 05458

First Edition

ISBN: 978-1-950040-00-1 (paperback)

Post-Traumatic Stress Disorder

PTSD is a response to life-threatening trauma in which the victim continues to have psychological and physiological responses to reminders of the event (referred to as triggers) even after the individual has reached safety. This often includes hyper-vigilance (constantly scanning for possible threats), intense anxiety or panic attacks, nightmares and flashbacks, exaggerated startle response, and numbing of emotions. At their worst, these symptoms can be completely debilitating, and lead many to commit, or at least consider, suicide; at best, they require the survivor to learn to navigate a mind and body that fundamentally work differently than they did before the trauma.

Over 5 million American adults are living with PTSD, and an estimated 7.8% of people in the U.S. will deal with PTSD symptoms at some point in their lives. Anyone can develop PTSD, but it often presents in people who have experienced physical or sexual violence, military combat, natural disasters, or serious accidents. While there is officially no cure, with the correct treatment survivors can learn to manage symptoms and drastically decrease their severity.

PTSD and Art

This gallery is the artist's response to her own journey with PTSD. The pieces reflect symptoms at various stages along the healing process. Her choice to make such a personal journey public stems from an underlying desire to help others who are suffering by providing education to those who may not understand, and hope to those who do.

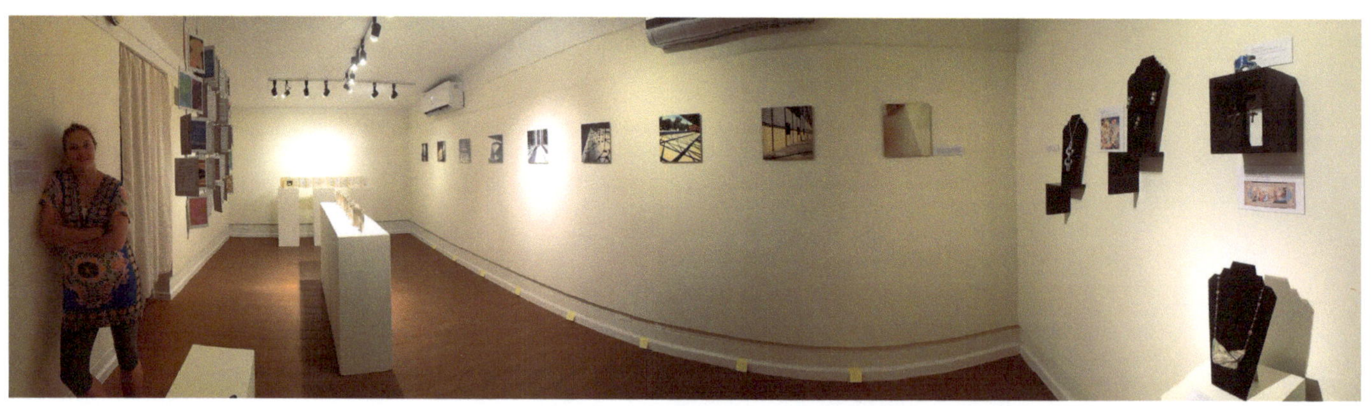

Gallery display at Isla Center for the Arts, Guam, 2018

Particularly in military circles, PTSD has been coined "an invisible wound of war". And it's very hard to fight what you cannot see. I'm just trying to make it easier to see. Then it's easier to fight. I don't care what your "war" was: whether you're suffering because you're a soldier, or because you were raped or in an abusive relationship, or anything else. All of us suffering from PTSD understand each other, so it makes sense to me that we support each other too.

- Kimberly Mann

It begins in darkness.

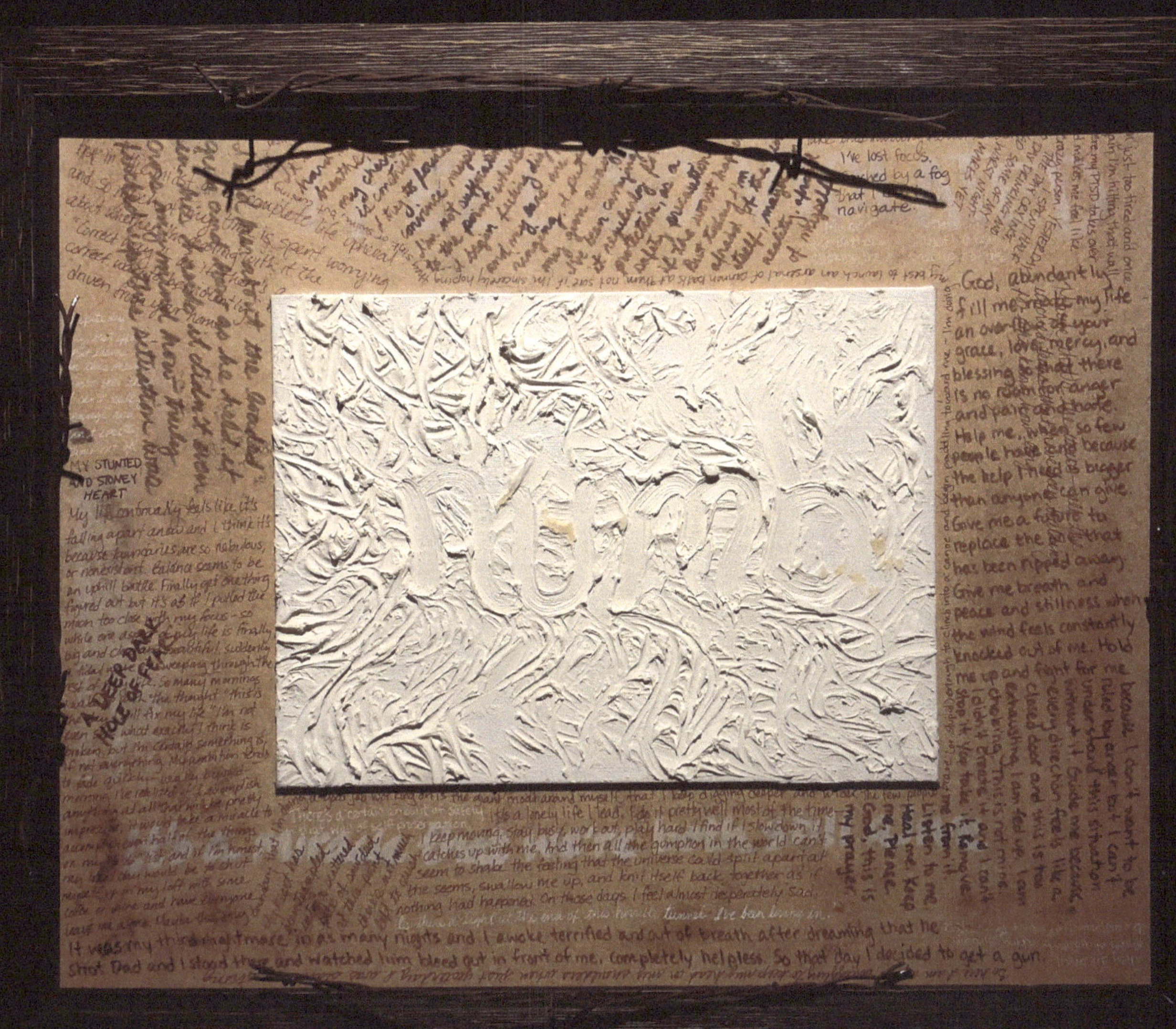

Numb, 2015 - 2018

Oil on canvas board with mixed media.
18.5 x 22.5 inches

One of the most common and difficult symptoms of Post-Traumatic Stress Disorder is the inability to feel. It prevents individuals from making new relationships, seeking help, or moving on from their pain. From the *DSM-IV*:

> Diminished responsiveness to the external world, referred to as "psychic numbing" or "emotional anesthesia," usually begins soon after the traumatic event. The individual may complain of having markedly diminished interest or participation in previously enjoyed activities, of feeling detached or estranged from other people, or of having markedly reduced ability to feel emotions (especially those related with intimacy, tenderness, and sexuality).

The painted portion of this piece was painted during a triggering episode. It was later matted and framed with texts from my journal.

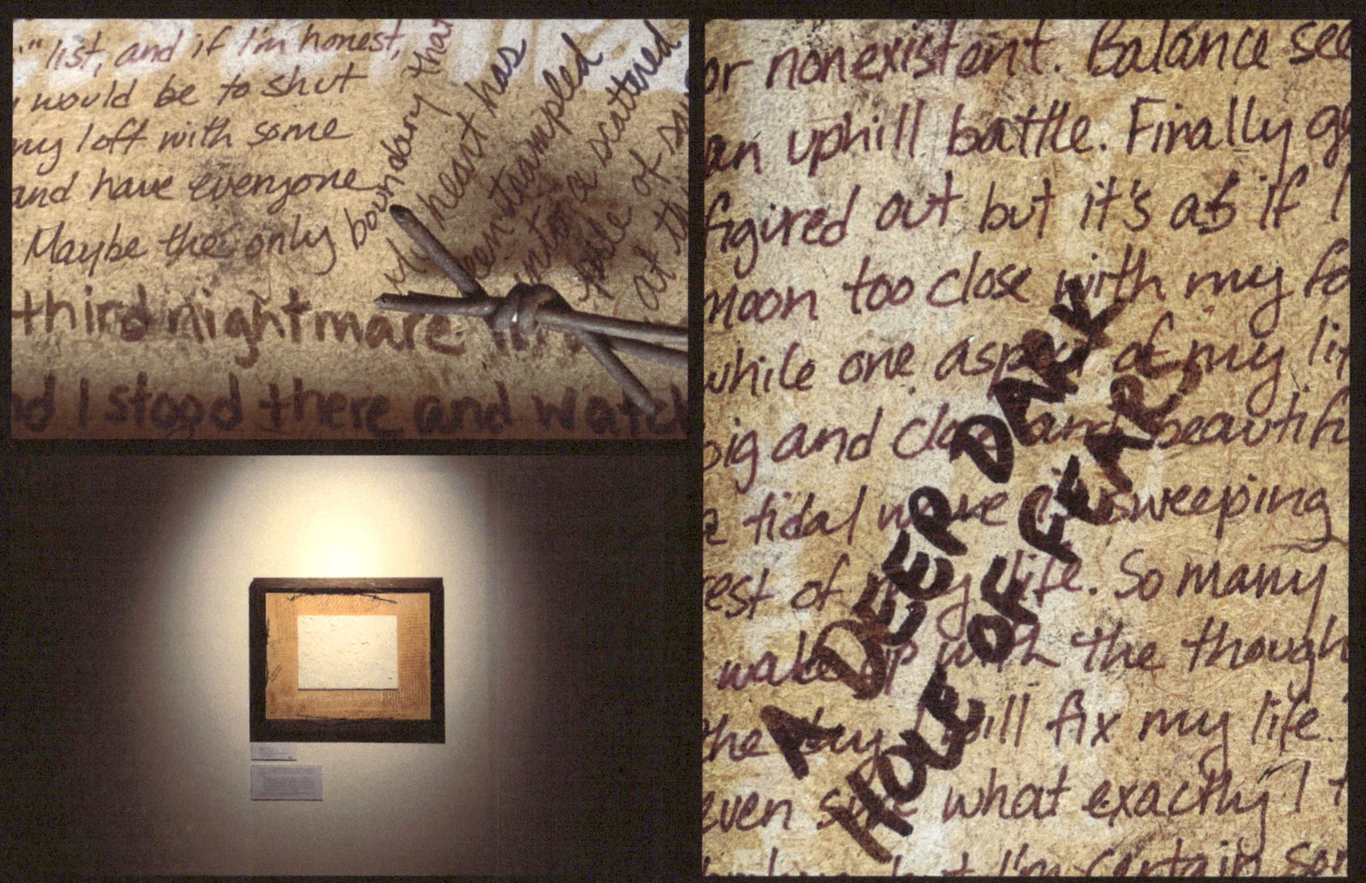

In a darkened room, viewers experience the isolation of the piece, *Numb*.

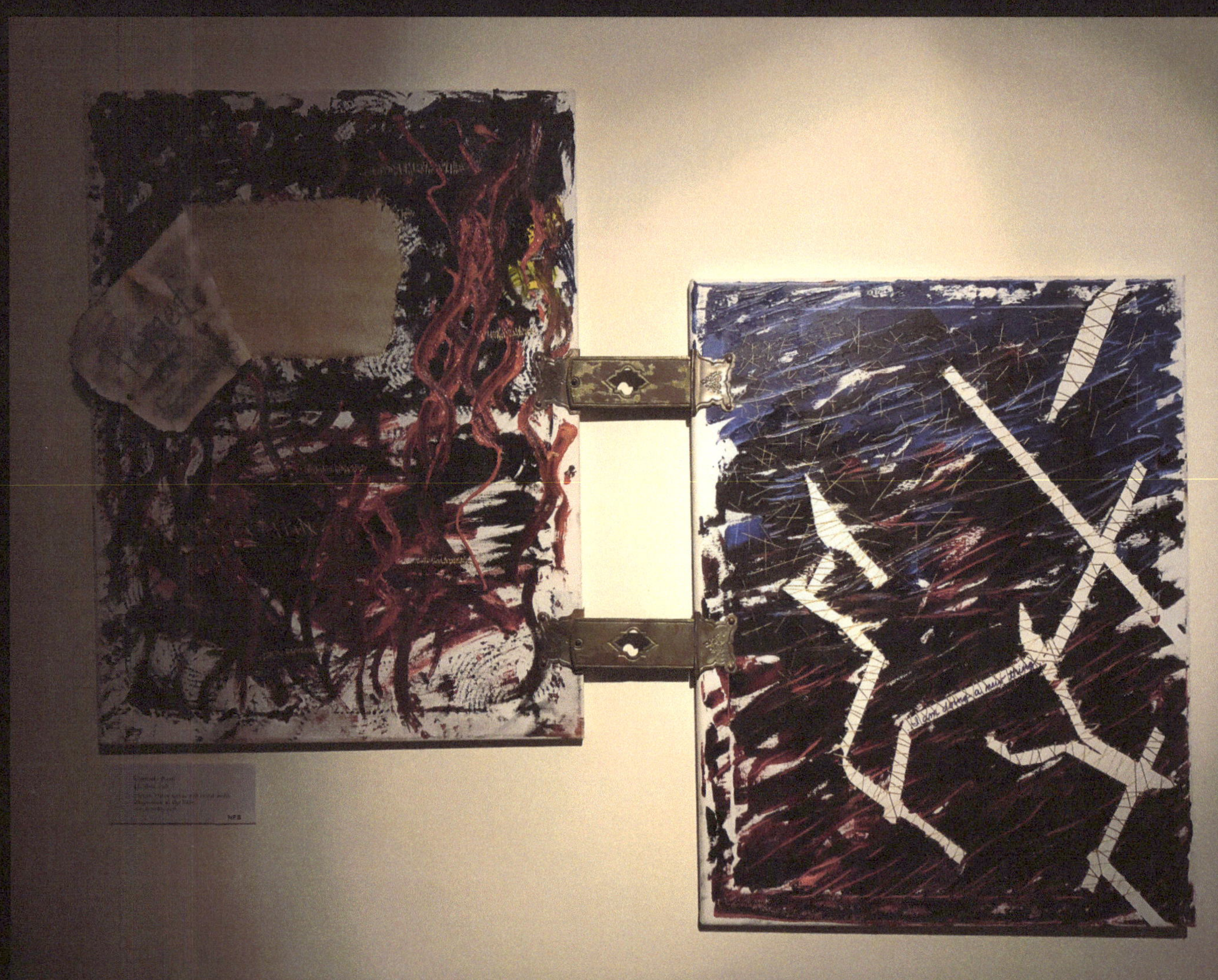

43, 2016 - 2018

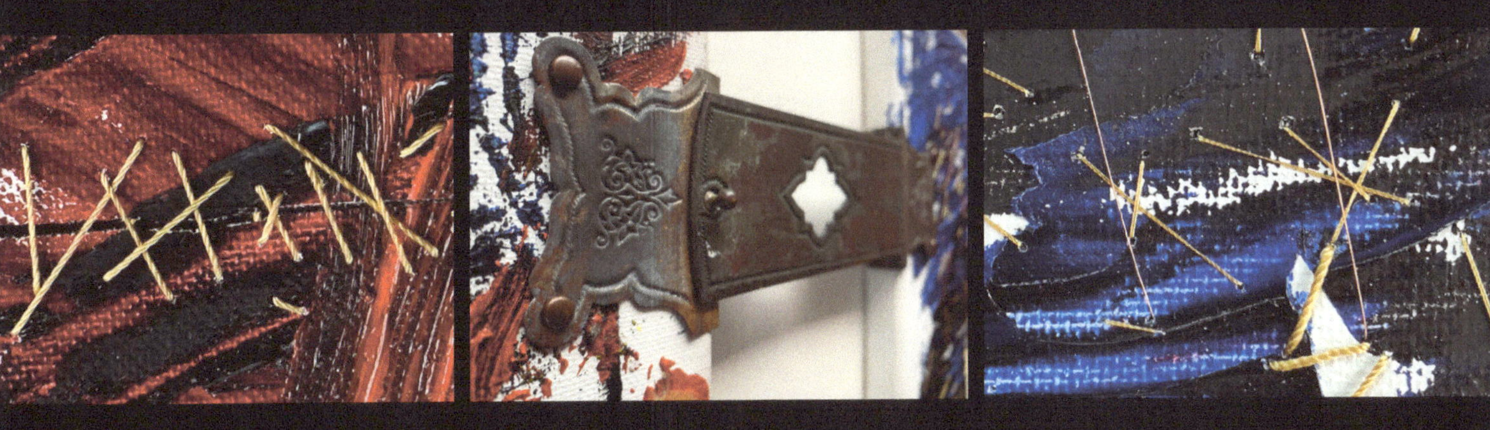

Purposely obscured in shadow, this piece exudes the pain
and chaos of a broken life…

The first canvas of the diptych was painted during a triggering episode, after which, in my anger, I punched a hole through. Two years later, new fabric was sewn into the hole, representing the clean slate available to us when we allow God to cleanse our sin and heal our past. Something dark and ugly and broken can be turned into something light and beautiful and whole. Seven slashes in the canvas were sewn back together, representing seven lost years of my life that are healing, but have left scars.

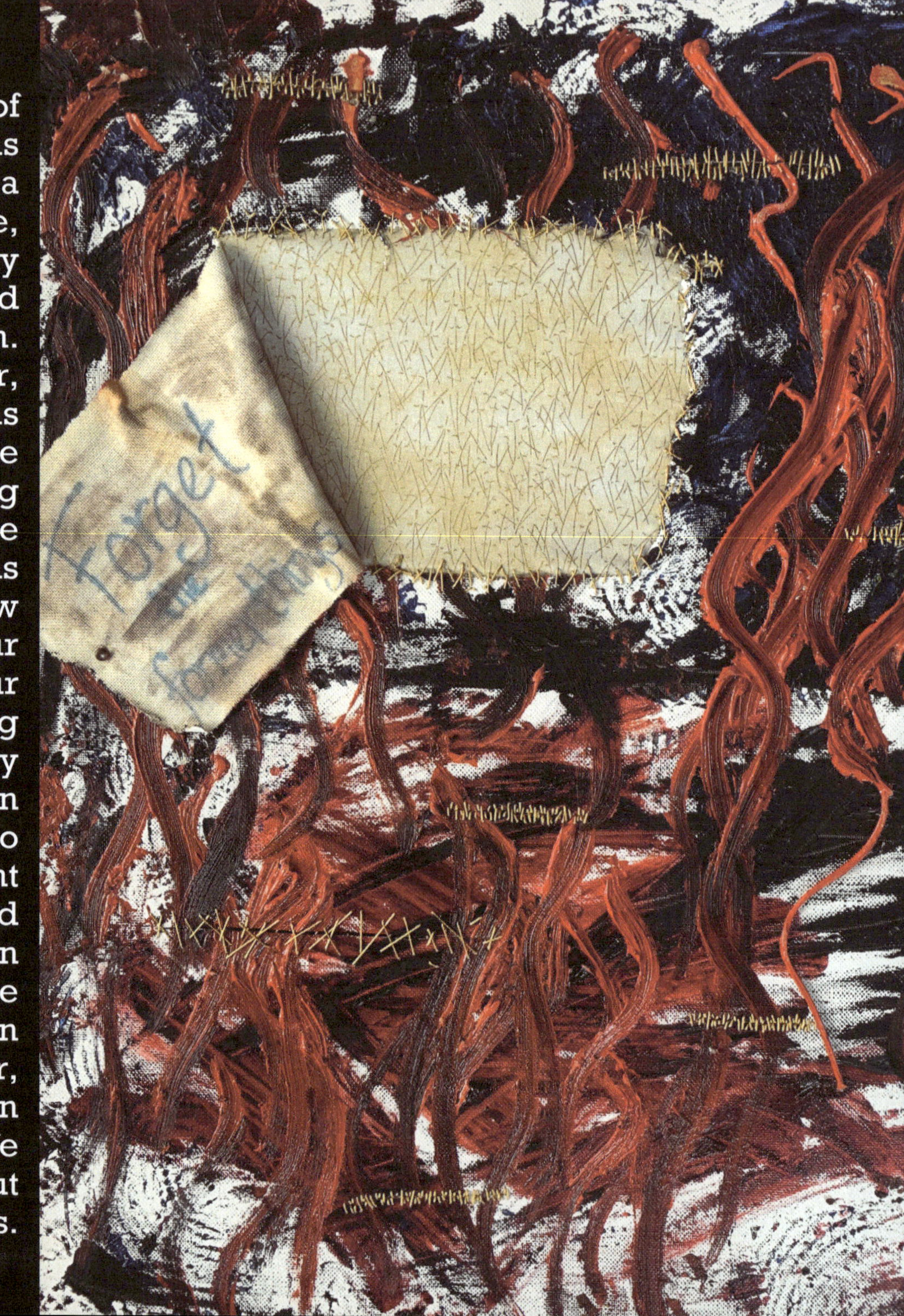

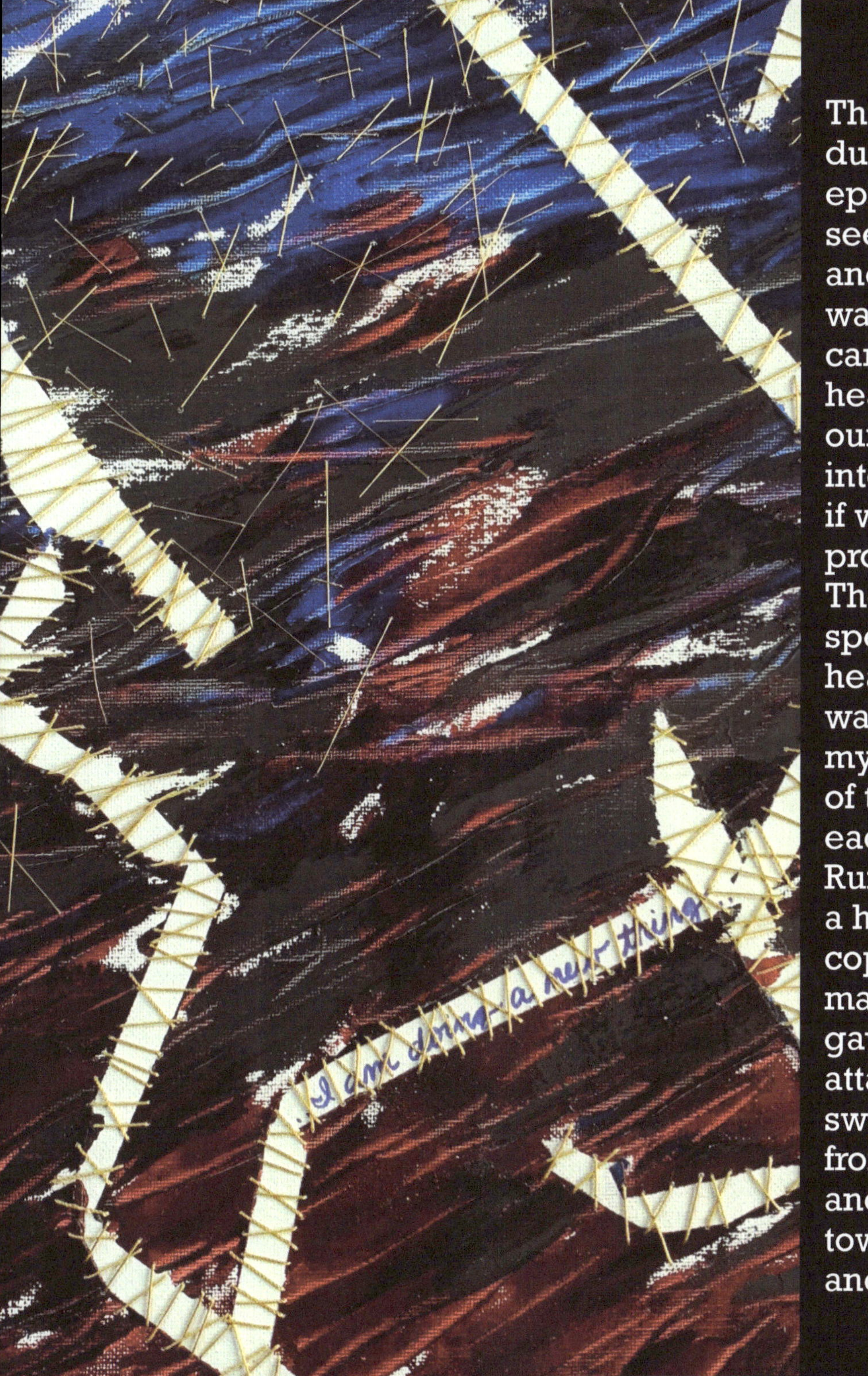

This canvas was painted during another triggering episode, when I couldn't see past the darkness and anger. Silk thread was later sewn into the canvas, representing the healing process and how our brokenness can turn into something beautiful if we allow that healing process to take place. The copper wire is more specific to my personal healing journey. The wire was pulled from one of my running bibs—part of the tracker that keeps each runner's pace. Running has become a healthy outlet and coping mechanism for managing my PTSD. It gave me a way to make attainable goals and switch from running away from something (danger and the past), to running toward something (goals and healing).

The first room of the gallery was meant to make people feel uncomfortable. We often ignore the things that make us uncomfortable, but those are the very things that need more attention. Without discomfort, we are complacent, unwilling to make necessary changes in our lives and in the world.

While I had never intended to publicly display these pieces—pieces made in my darkest hours—I realized they were crucial to the narrative. You can't fully comprehend the healing process unless you first get a feel for the pain and suffering. So, we had to start in the darkness. Thankfully, none of us have to stay there.

Forget the former things; do not dwell on the
past. See, I am doing a new thing! Now it springs
up; do you not perceive it? I am making a way
in the wilderness and streams in the wasteland.
— Isaiah 43:18 & 19, NIV

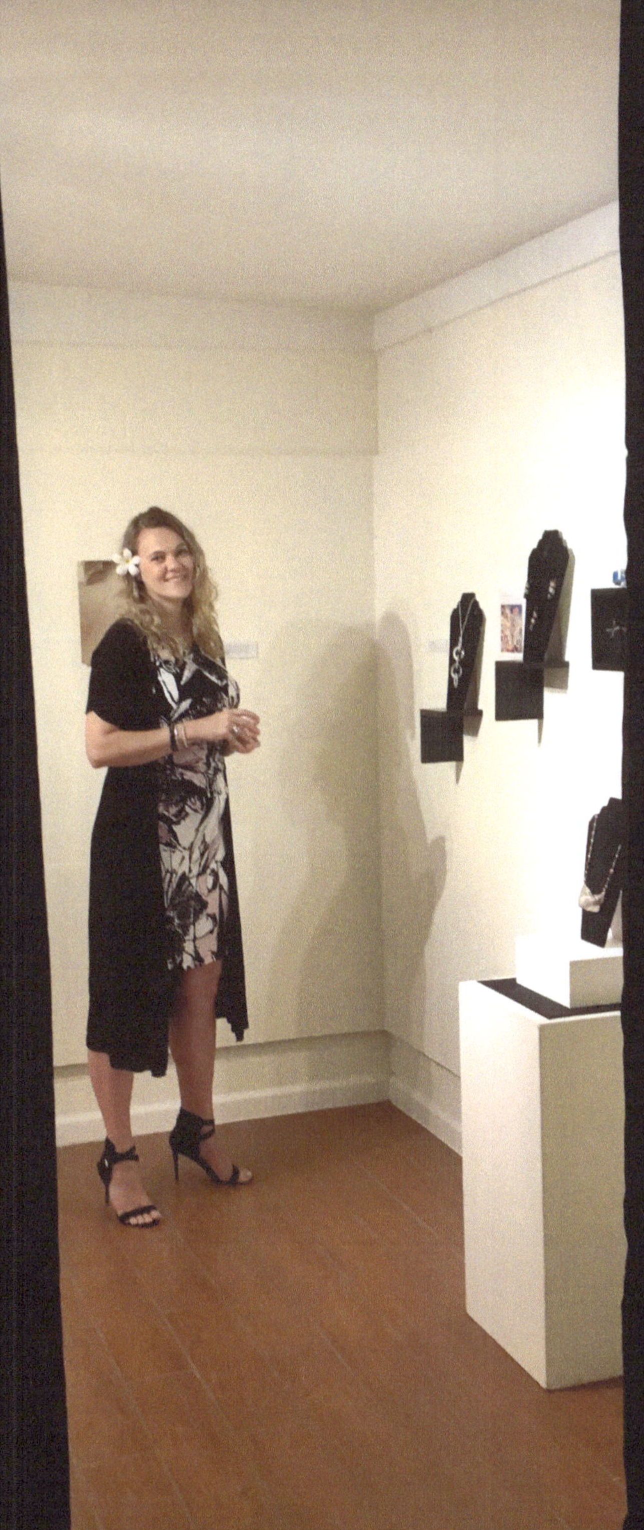

When the curtains open
from the blackened room,
the viewer is led into a
room full of light.

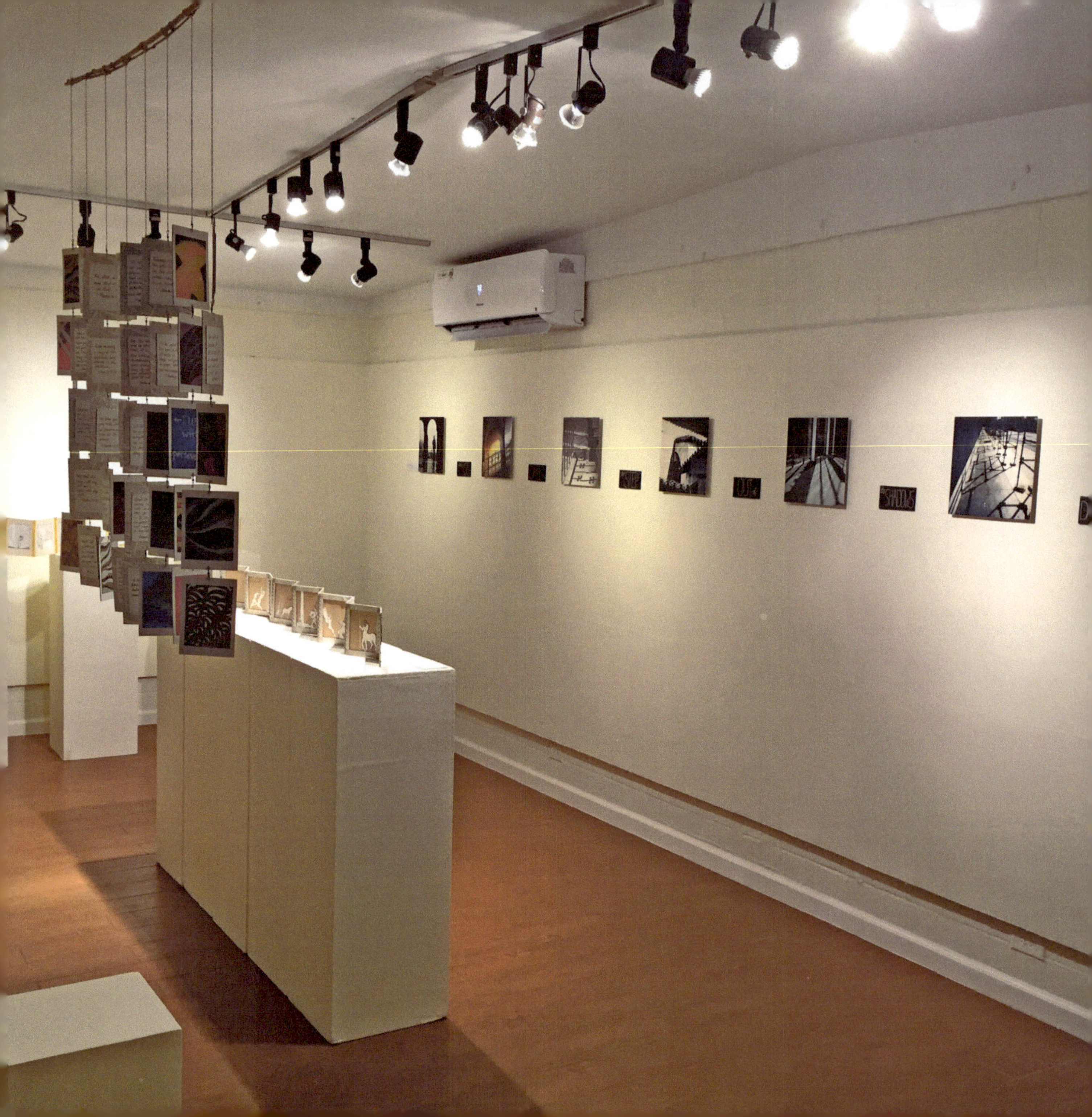

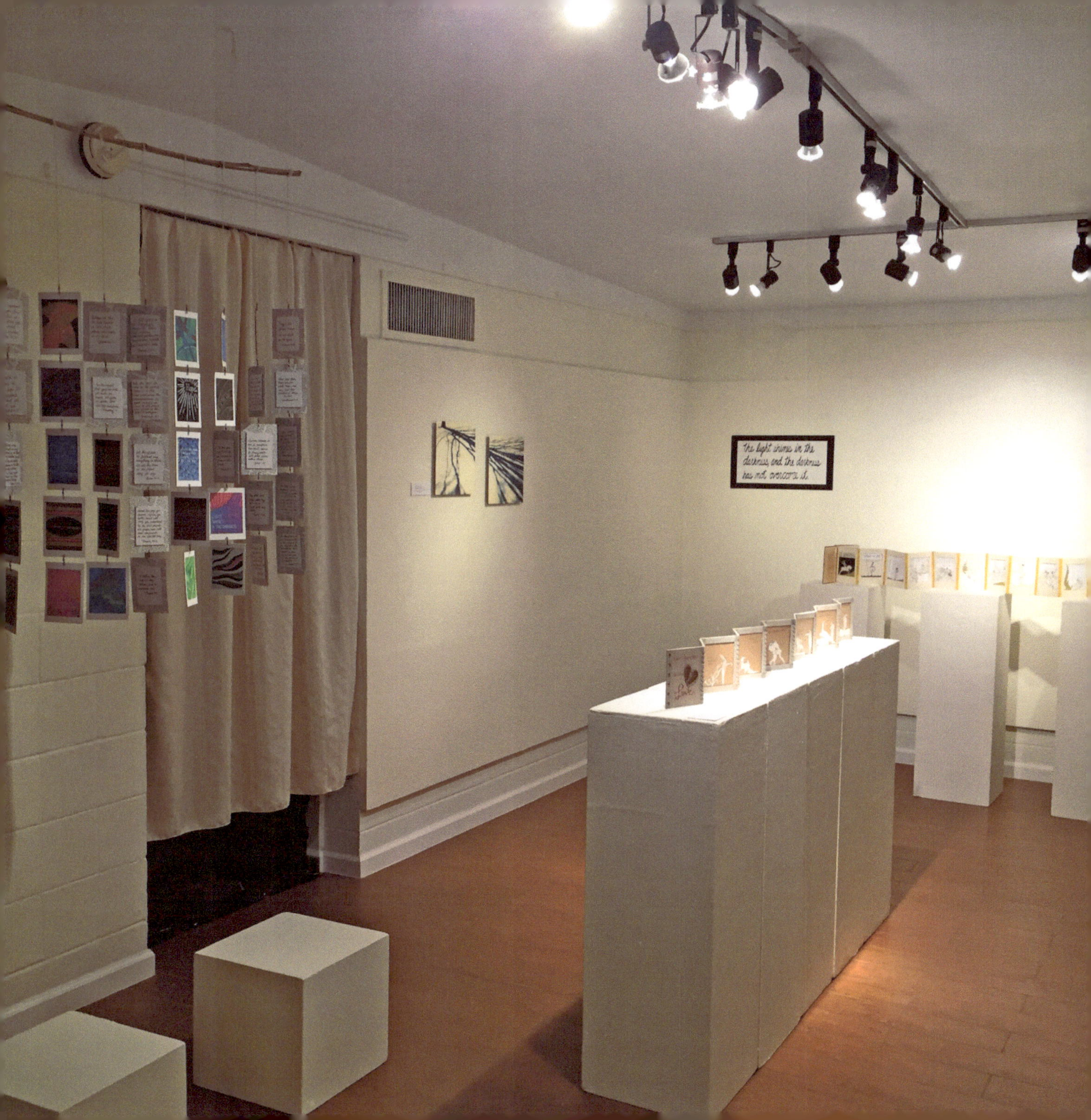
The light shines in the darkness, and the darkness has not overcome it.

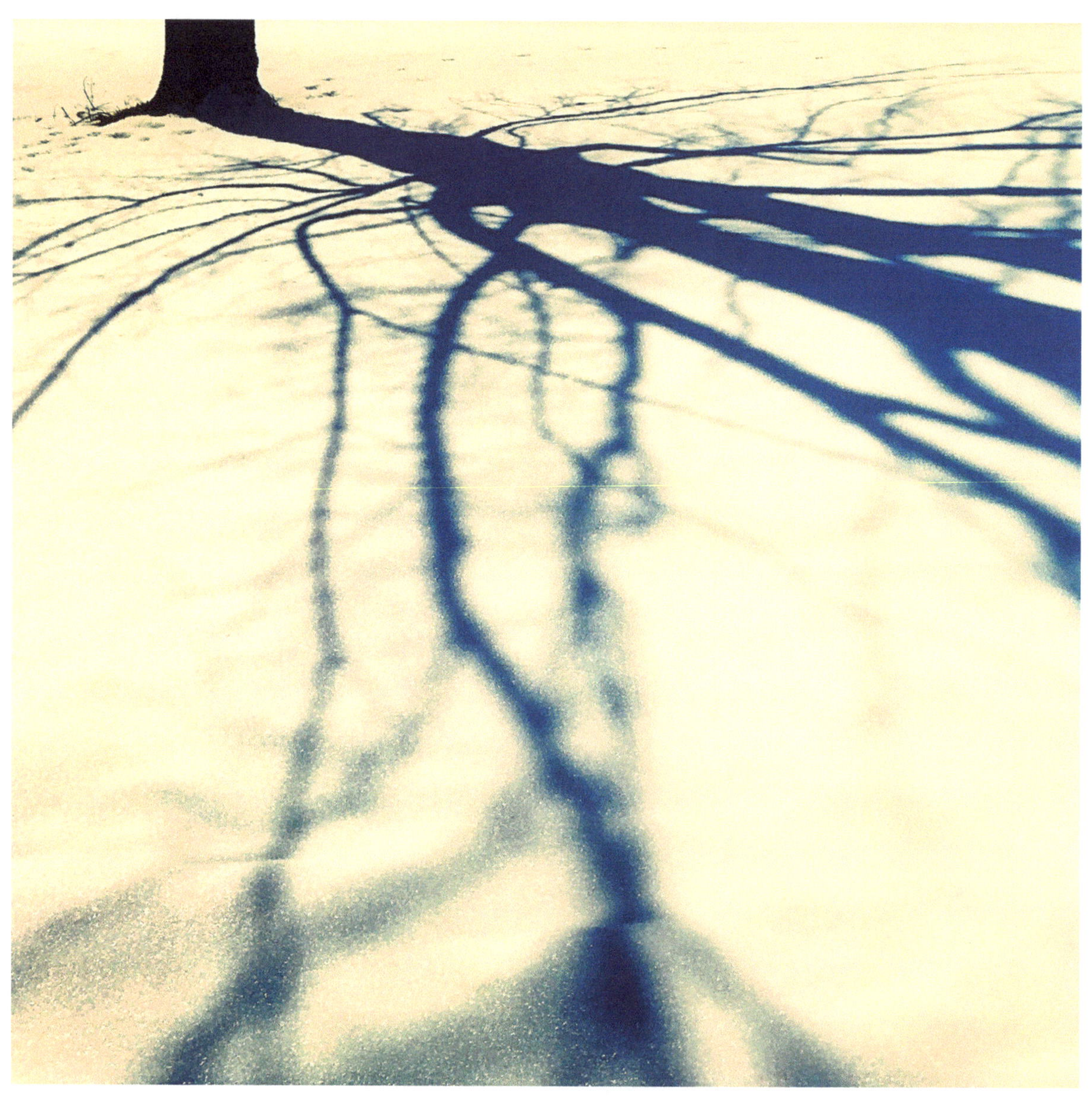

Shadows & Light II, 2018

Set of digital photographs printed on aluminum.
12 x 12 inches each

Illuminated by the light of the second room of the gallery
are themes of growth, healing, and hope.

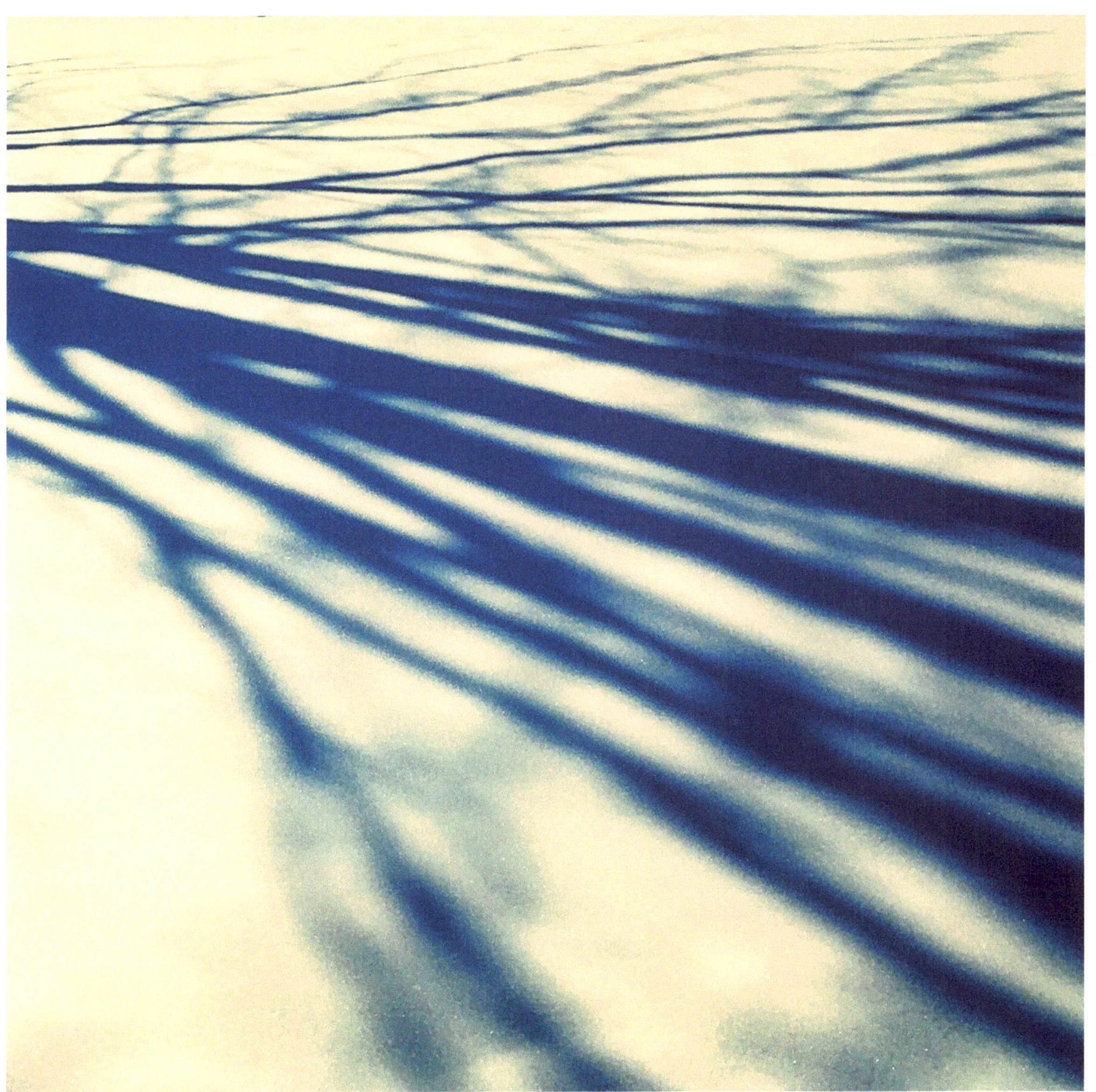

Rescued Remnants

This series of jewelry began after completing a different art piece, as I was cleaning my studio. I had carved a book and was throwing all the discarded pieces in the trash. Some illustrations caught my eye and I couldn't bring myself to leave them there, so I rescued them from out of the trash.

The resulting piece became the necklace, *Wild*, which has become one of my favorite pieces. From that point on, I've saved the scraps from each of my projects, turning them instead into a thing of beauty.

I've found this process to be comforting. There was a time, not too long ago, when I felt discarded—my world had crumbled around me, and the scraps of my former life didn't seem salvageable. Thankfully, that wasn't the end. With time, healing, and the overwhelming grace of God, I've been plucked from the trash, dusted off, and made new. The small remnant of my broken life was rescued and is daily being glued back together—not back to what it was, but it's being transformed into a beautifully new and distinctive creation.

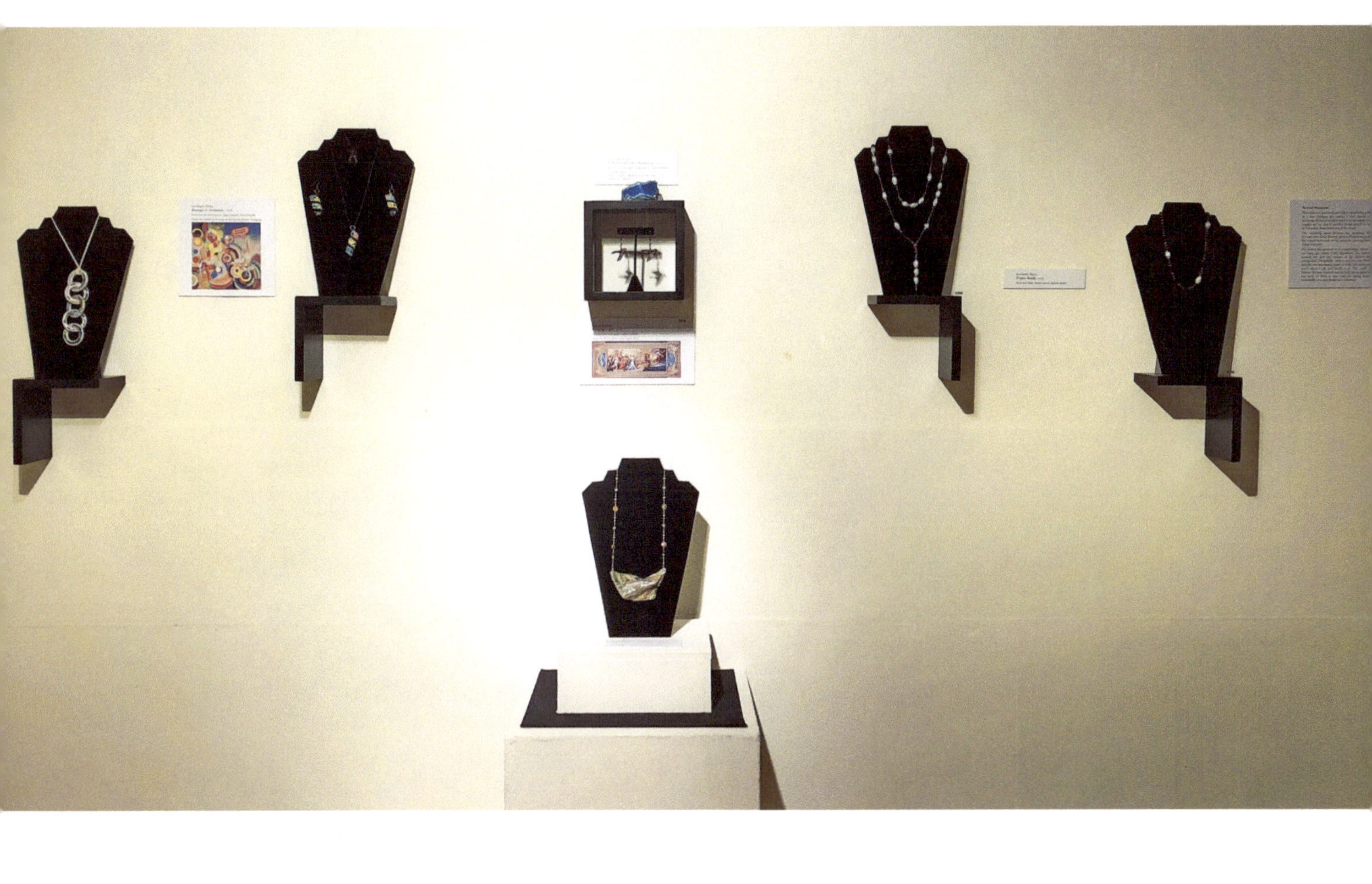

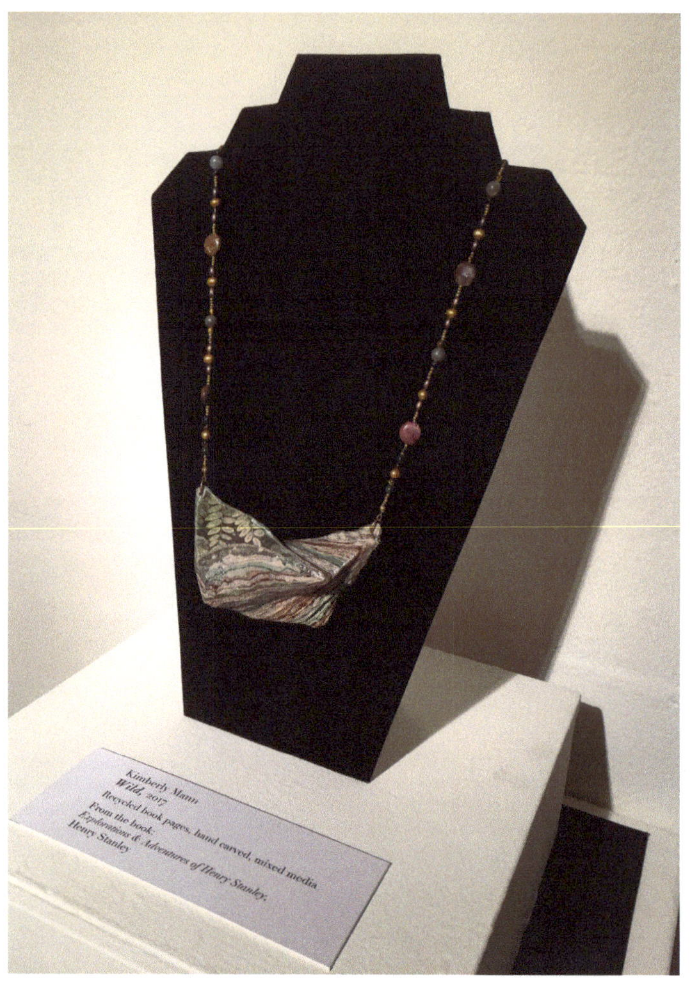

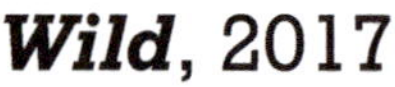

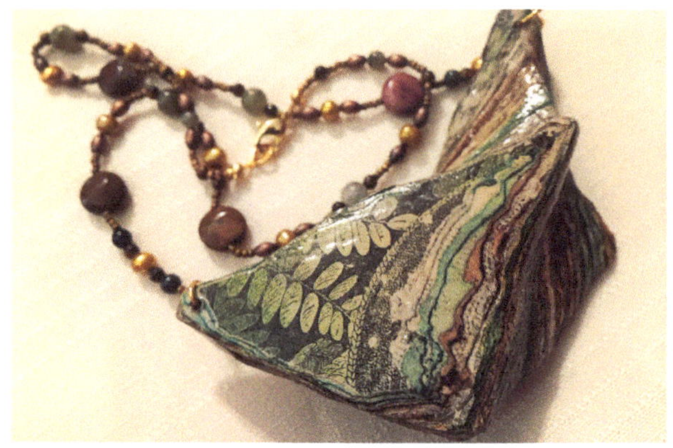

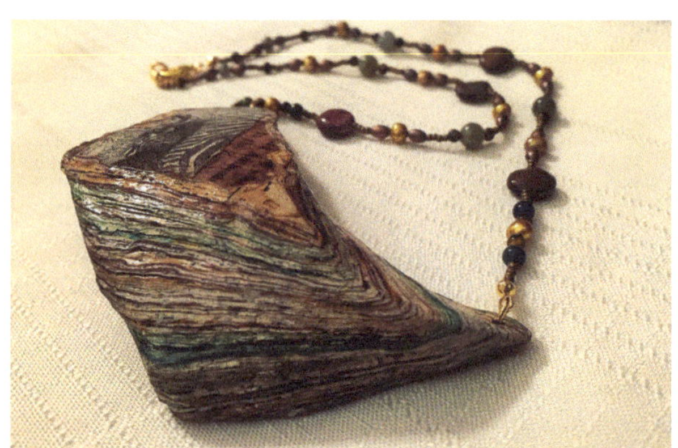

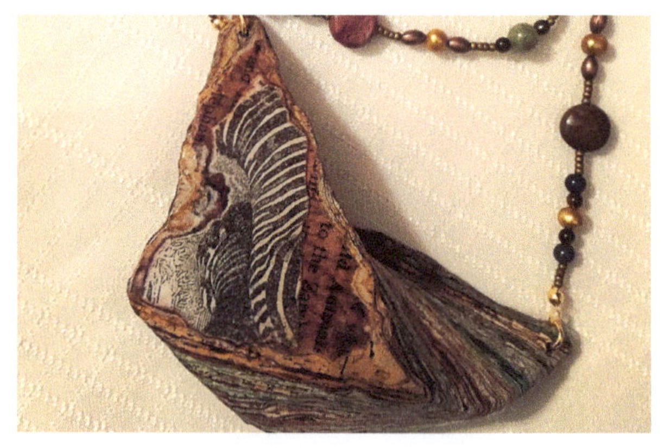

Wild, 2017

Recycled book pages, colored and glued, hand carved, sealed with acrylic medium. Strung with various beads on silk cord.

From the book, *Explorations & Adventures of Henry Stanley,* by Henry Stanley

From the 1614 fresco, *Aurora,* by Guido Reni

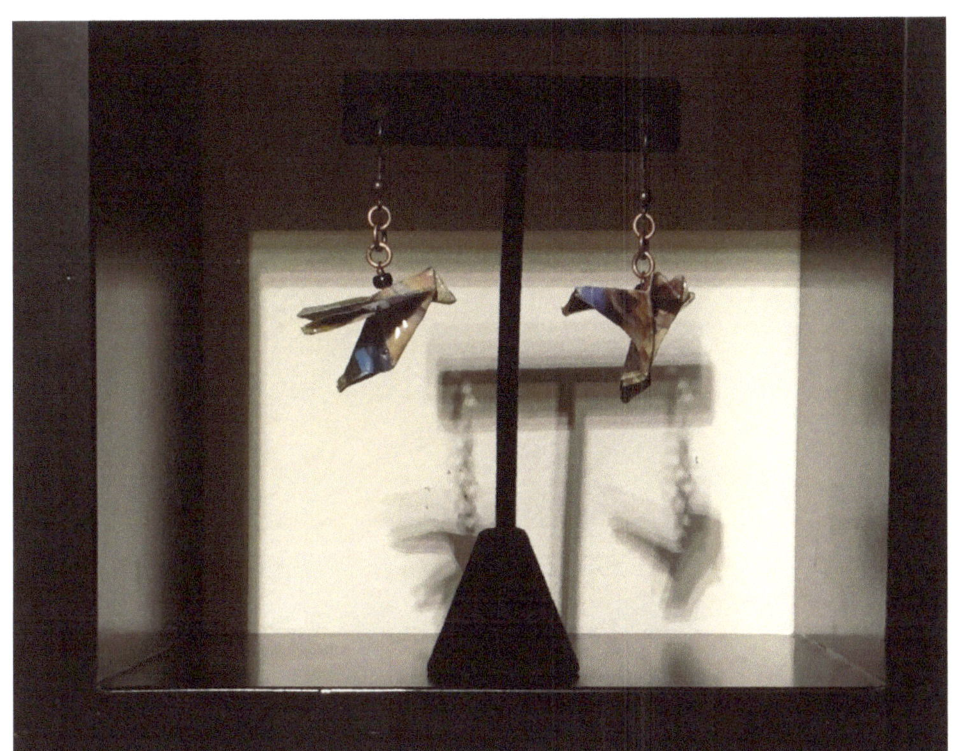

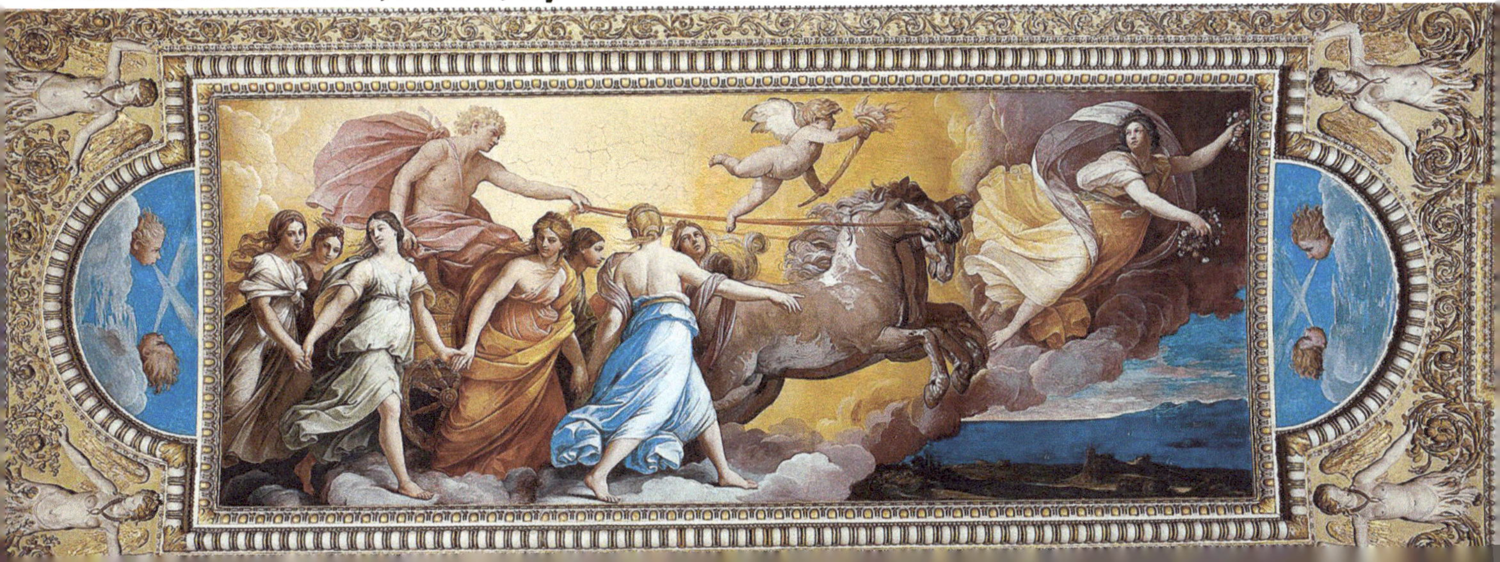

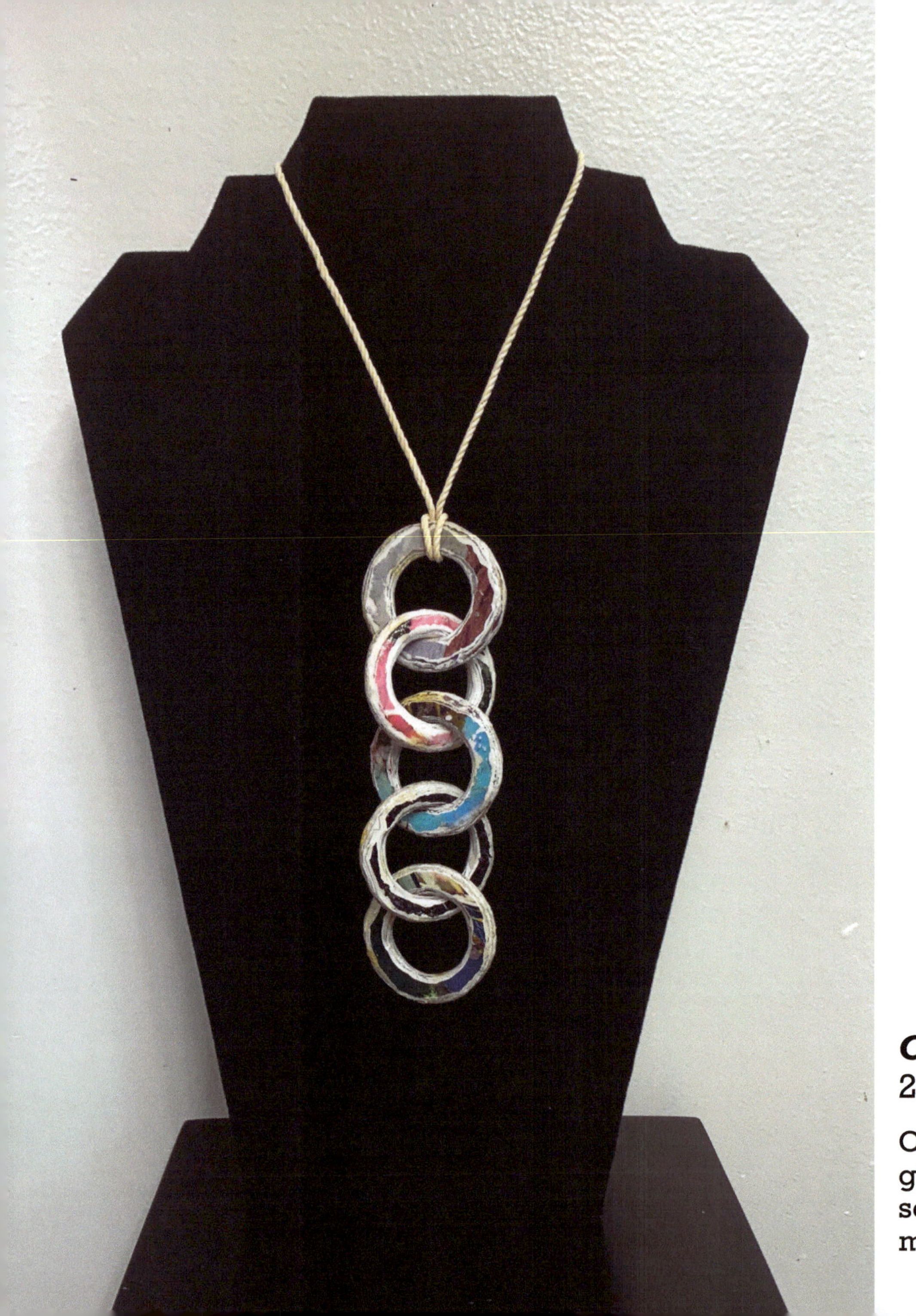

Chains of the Past
2017

Old wedding photos glued, hand carved, sealed with acrylic medium.

Homage to Delaunay
2018

Recycled art book pages
and acid-free paper,
glued, hand carved,
sealed with acrylic
medium.

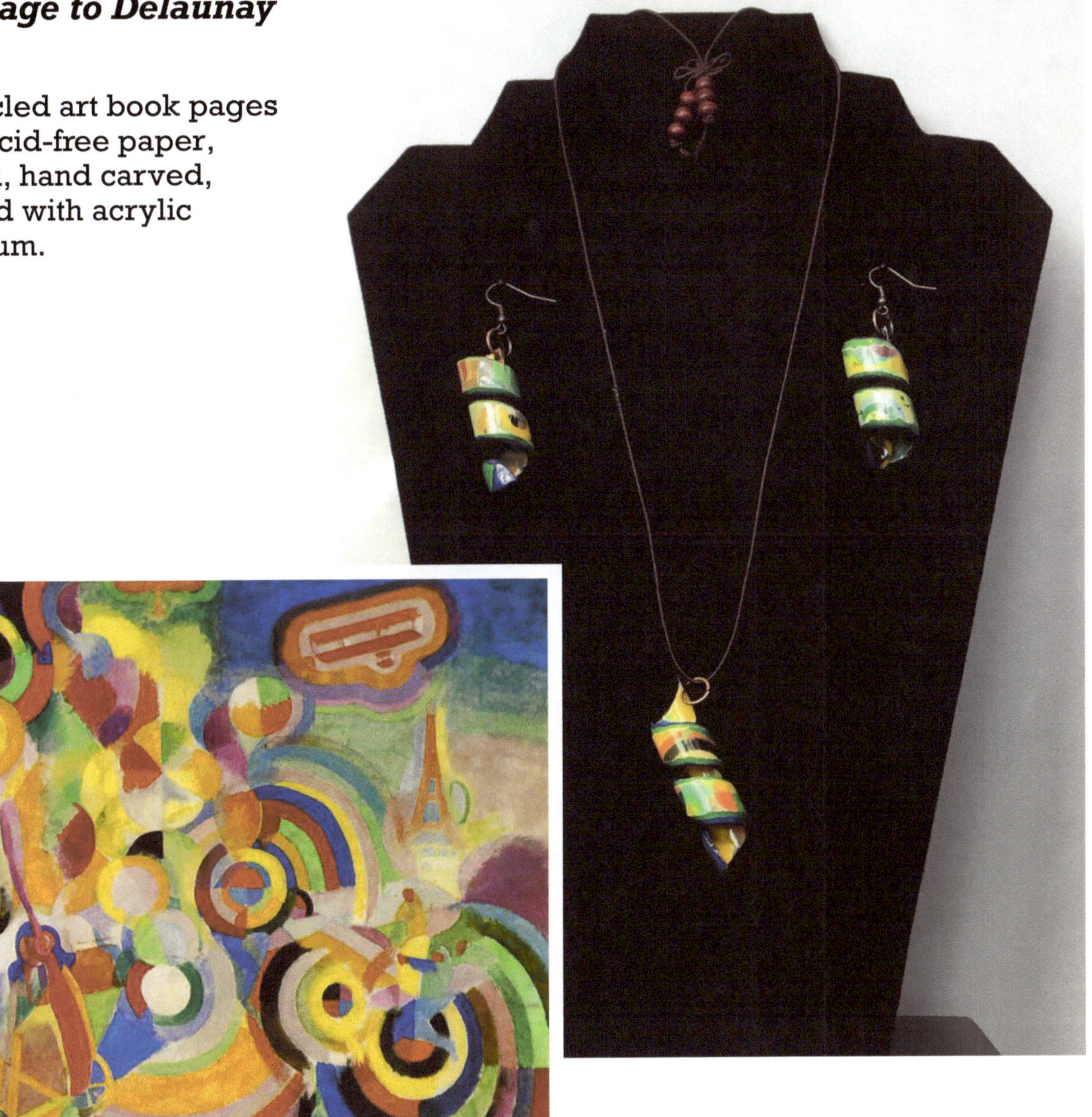

From the 1914 painting, *Homage to Bleriot*, by Robert Delaunay

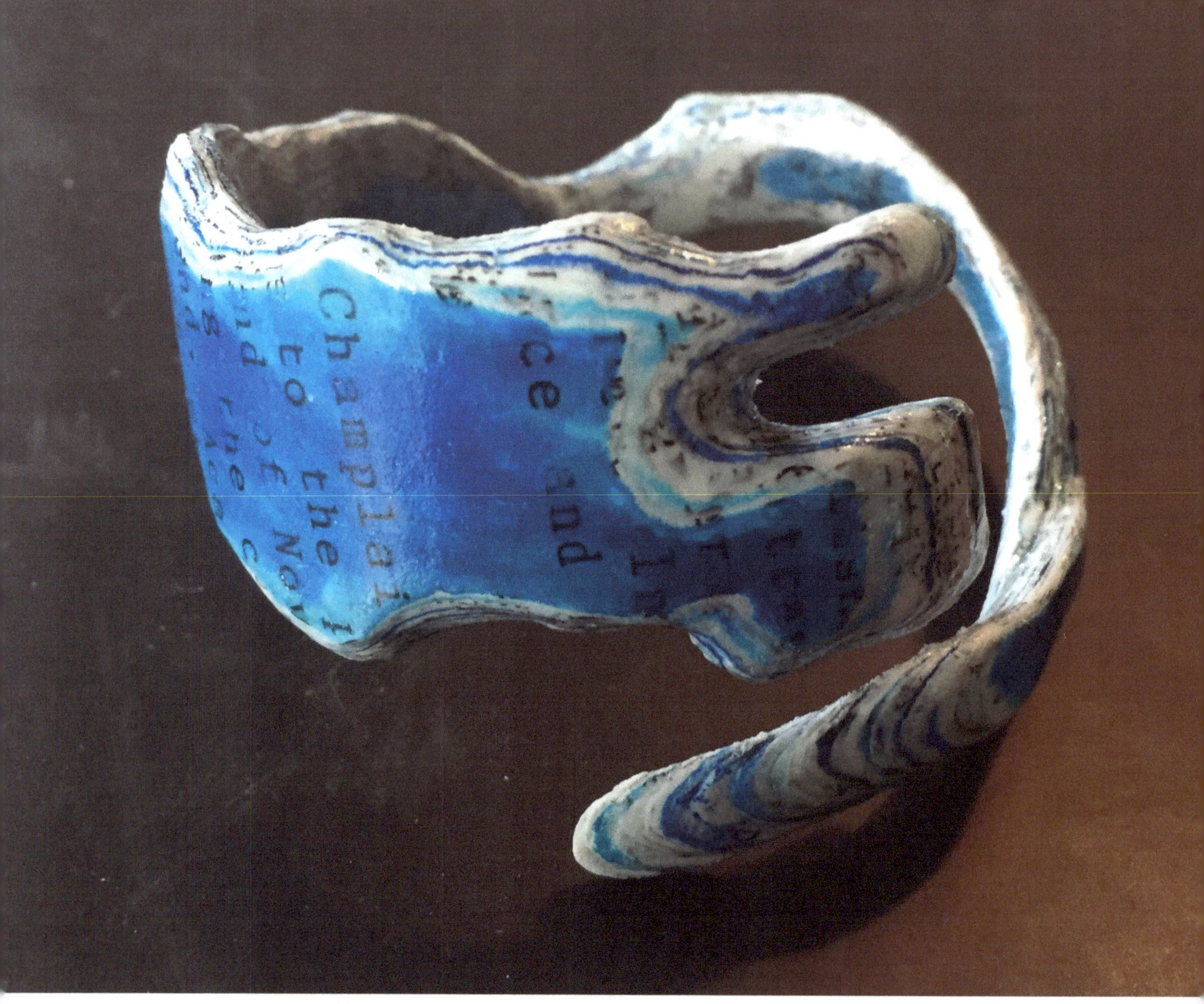

A History of Lake Champlain, 2017

Recycled book pages, colored and glued, hand carved, sealed with acrylic medium.
From the book, *Lake Champlain: Reflections on Our Past*, by Jennie G. Versteeg

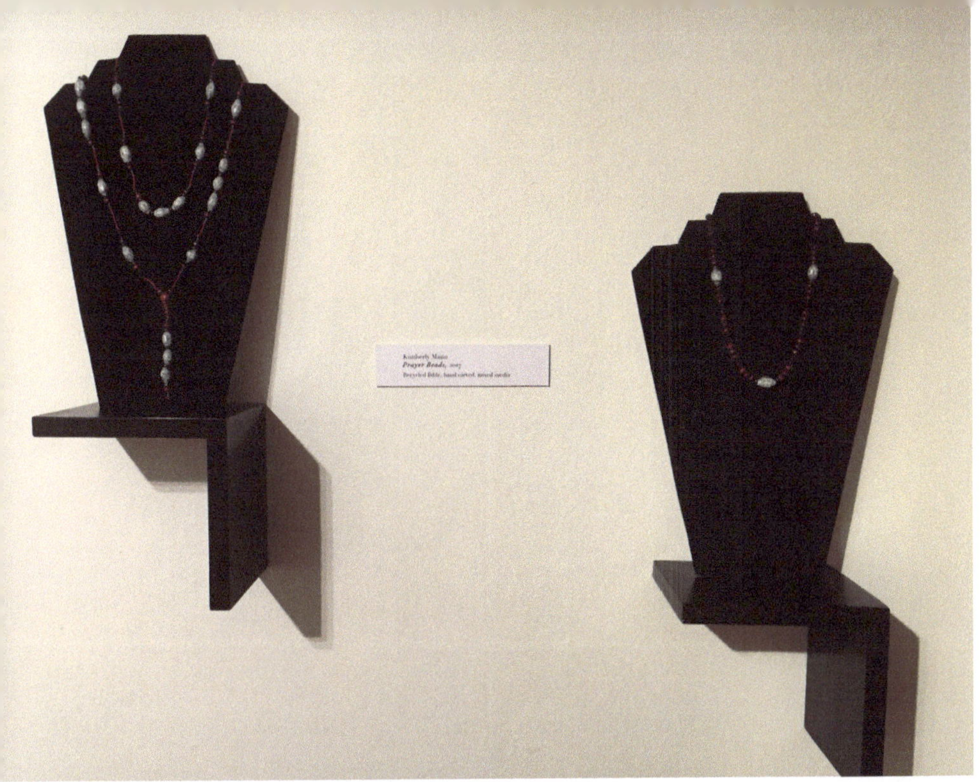

Prayer Beads, 2018

Recycled Bible pages glued, hand carved, sealed with acrylic medium. Strung with garnet stones and wooden beads on silk cord.

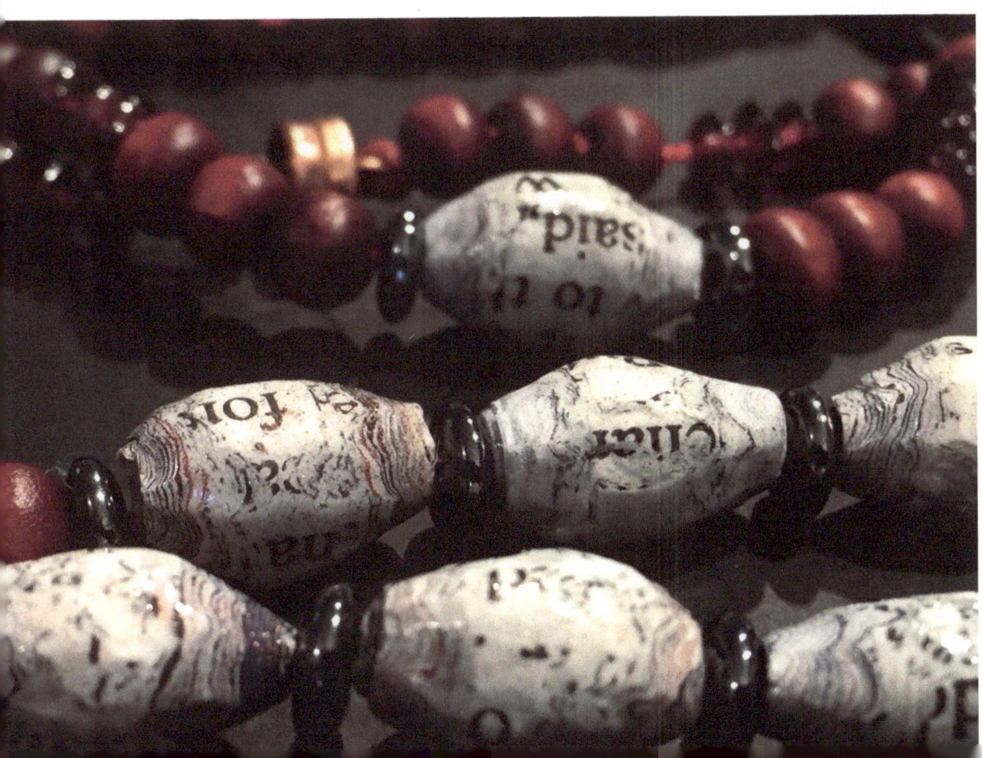

Lent Calendar, 2017

Recycled Bible, archival watercolor paper, mat board, oil paint markers, rolling barrel swivels, ceiling hooks and cotter pins. Displayed on rods of bamboo.

30 x 26 inches (approximately)

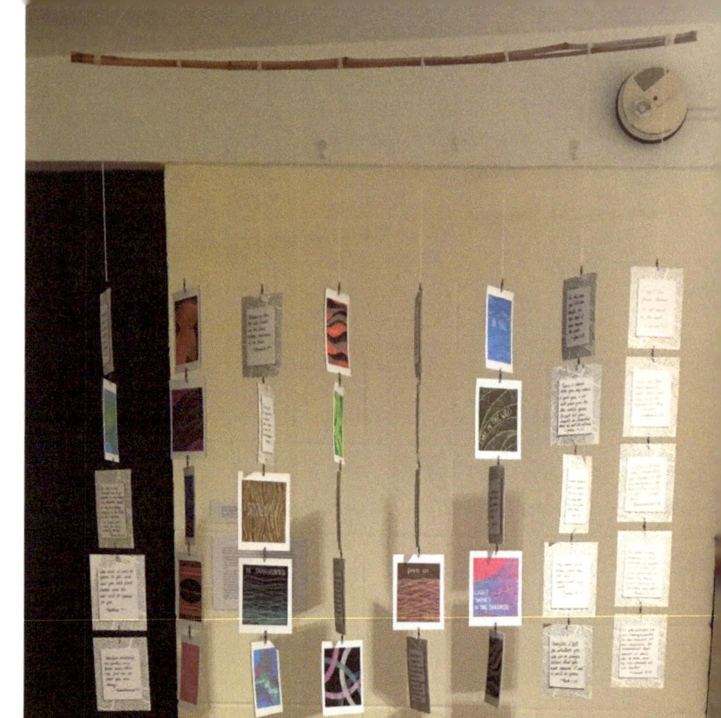

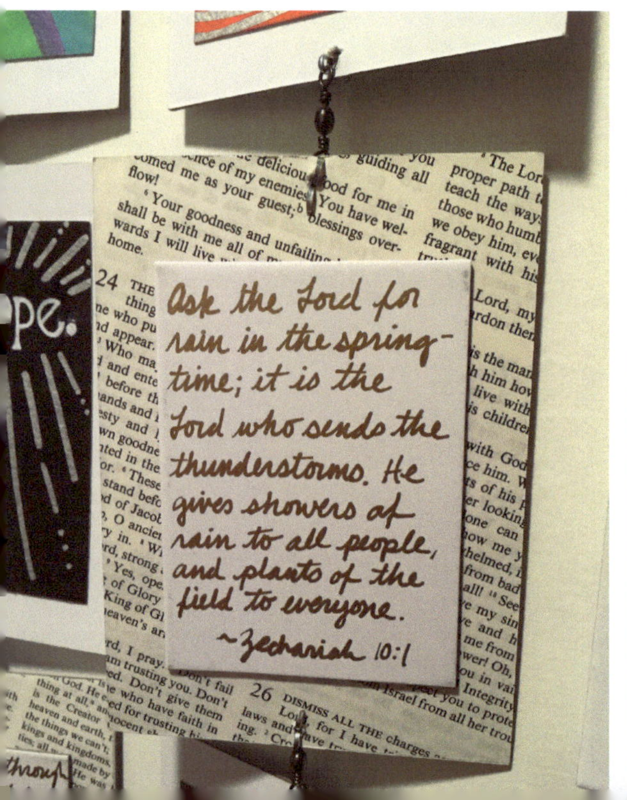

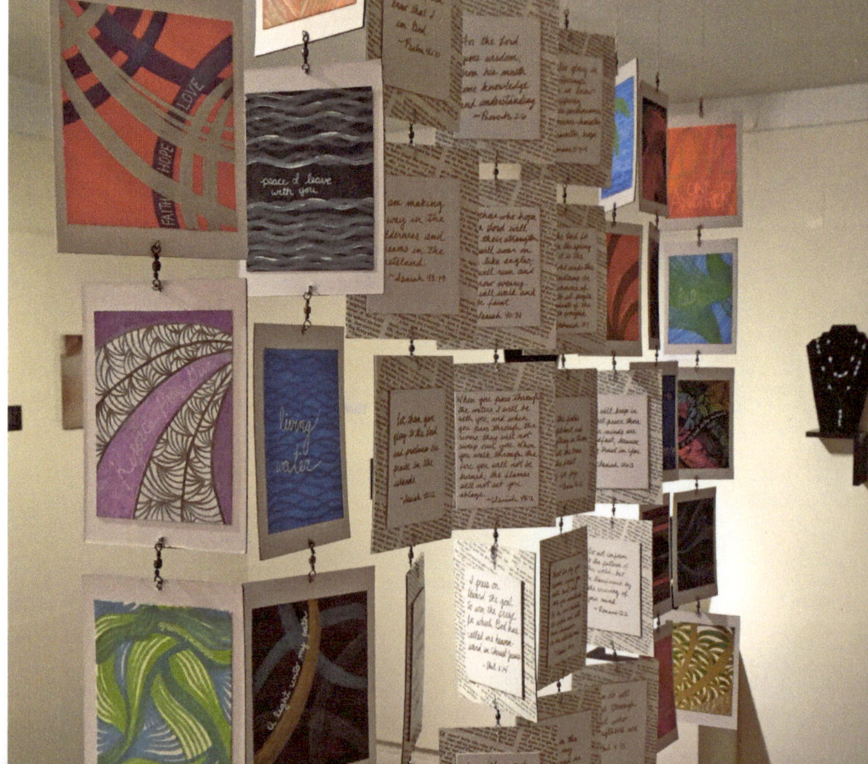

This was the first piece that got me back into art. After the culmination of my trauma and diagnosis, I avoided art because it felt too emotional. I was afraid of what emotions may come pouring out.

A friend had challenged those of us in a small group to find a unique way of observing Lent (the 40 days leading up to Easter), encouraging us that such an intentional meditation practice would be beneficial to our faith and wellbeing. I decided to use this challenge as an opportunity to return to art.

I cut 40 small pieces of watercolor paper and set aside a small case of markers, determining to fill my mini panels each day of Lent. The small size and limited number of art supplies felt less overwhelming than my previous attempts to return to art. The first day I did a piece in response to a Bible verse that had been a key source of hope in my life. When I finished the piece, I wrote the verse on the back. After that, I stuck with it, each day reflecting on another verse as I did my drawing. After Easter, I decided to turn the 40 drawings into a single piece, creating the *Lent Calendar*. Each panel rotates individually, allowing one to view either the image or text side. I loaned the piece to my friend from small group, who used it for Lent this year.

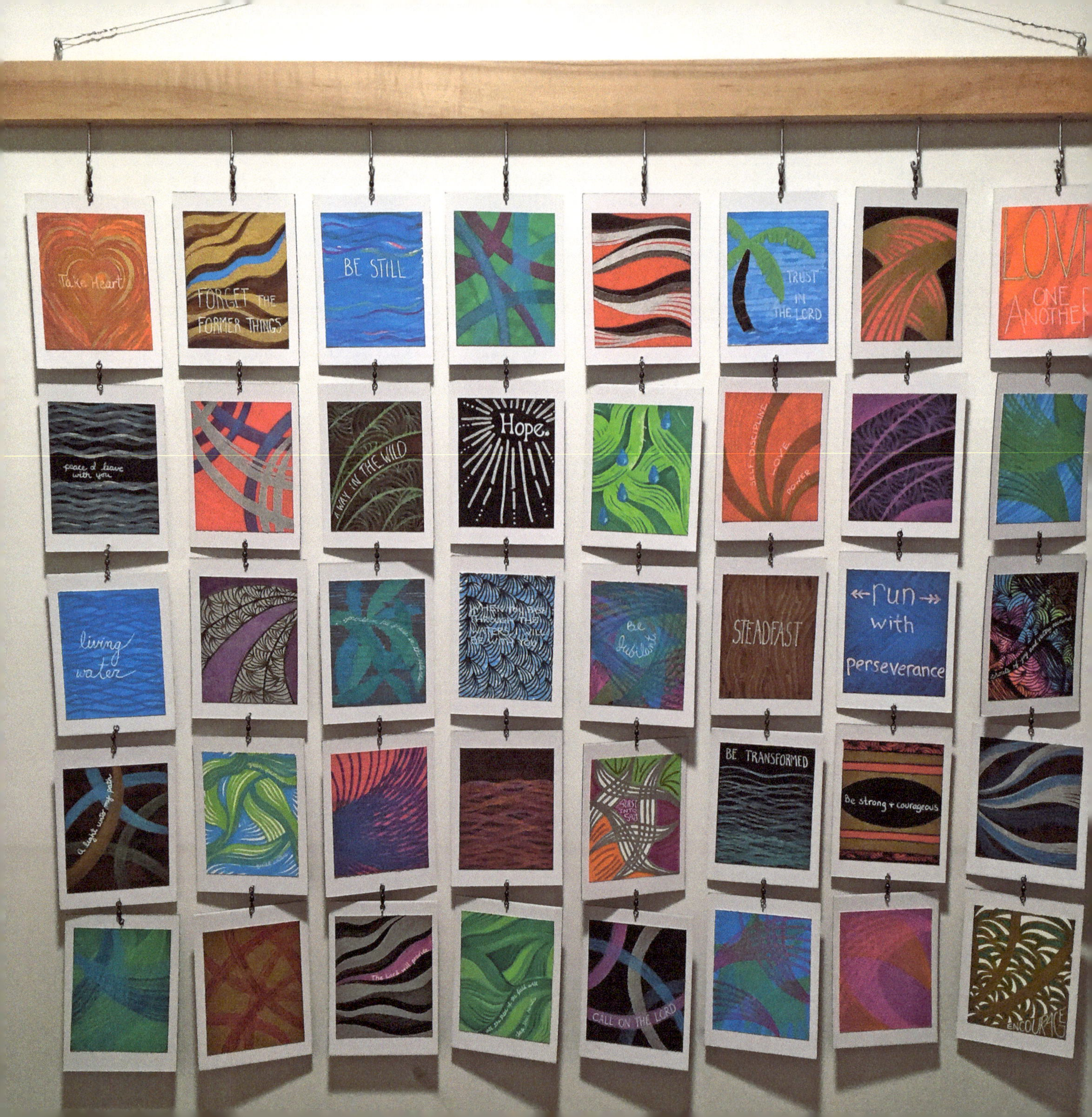
Take Heart
FORGET the FORMER THINGS
BE STILL
TRUST IN THE LORD
LOVE ONE ANOTHER
peace I leave with you
A WAY IN THE WILD
Hope.
SELF-DISCIPLINE LOVE POWER
living water
BE STEADFAST
←run→ with perseverance
Be jubilant
a light unto my path
BURST INTO SONG
BE TRANSFORMED
Be strong + courageous
The Lord will provide
CALL ON THE LORD
ENCOURAGE

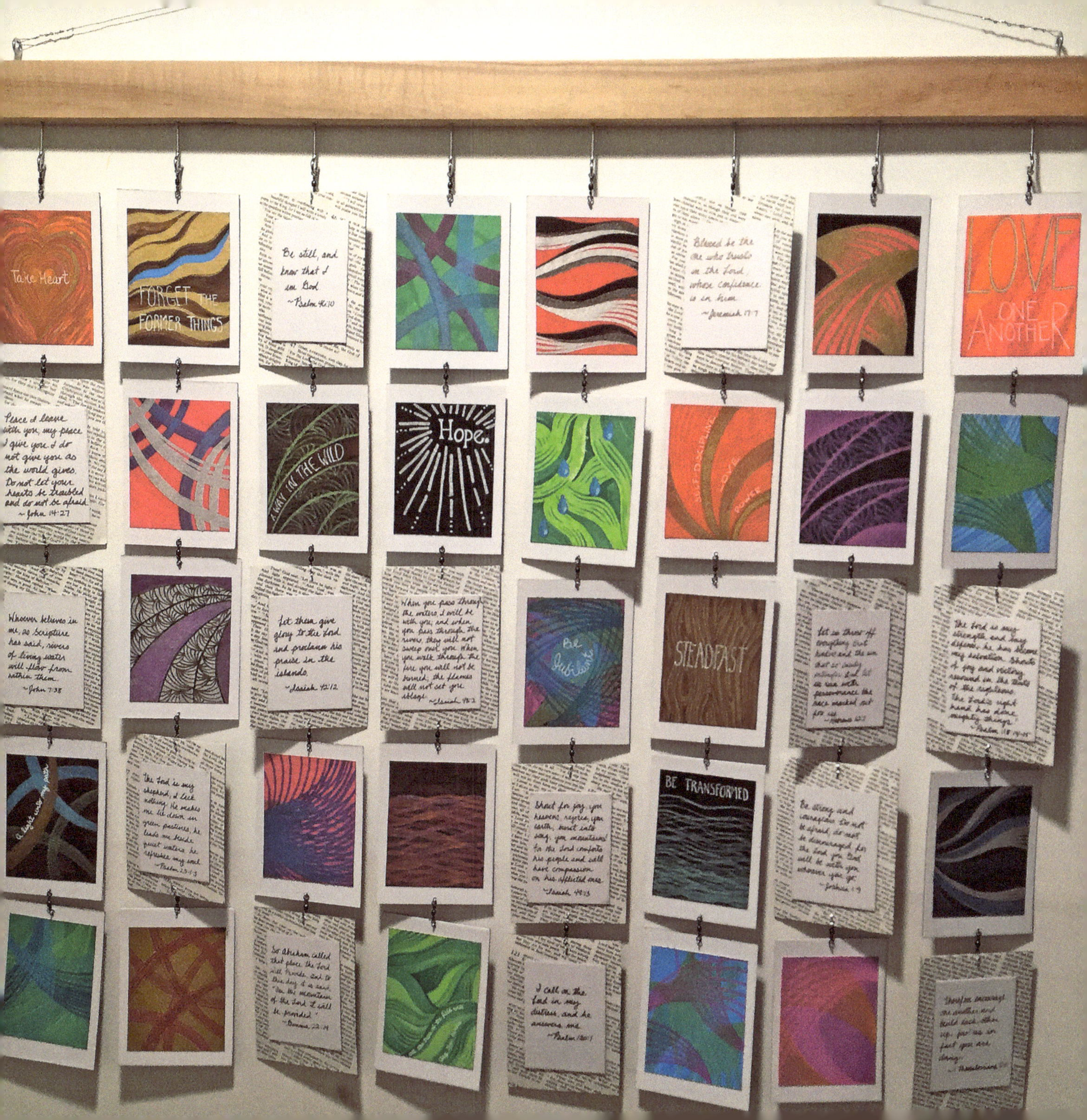

Take Heart
FORGET the FORMER THINGS
Be still, and know that I am God ~Psalm 46:10
Blessed be the one who trusts in the Lord, whose confidence is in him. ~Jeremiah 17:7
LOVE ONE ANOTHER
Peace I leave with you, my peace I give you. I do not give you as the world gives. Do not let your hearts be troubled and do not be afraid. ~John 14:27
A WAY IN THE WILD
Hope.
When you pass through the waters I will be with you; and when you pass through the rivers, they will not sweep over you. When you walk through the fire you will not be burned; the flames will not set you ablaze. ~Isaiah 43:2
Whoever believes in me, as scripture has said, rivers of living water will flow from within them. ~John 7:38
Let them give glory to the Lord and proclaim his praise in the islands. ~Isaiah 42:12
Be Jubilant
STEADFAST
The Lord is my strength and my defense; he has become my salvation.
BE TRANSFORMED
Be strong and courageous. Do not be afraid; do not be discouraged, for the Lord your God will be with you wherever you go. ~Joshua 1:9
The Lord is my shepherd, I lack nothing. He makes me lie down in green pastures, he leads me beside quiet waters, he refreshes my soul. ~Psalm 23:1-3
Shout for joy, you heavens; rejoice, you earth; burst into song, you mountains! For the Lord comforts his people and will have compassion on his afflicted ones. ~Isaiah 49:13
So Abraham called that place The Lord Will Provide. And to this day it is said, "On the mountain of the Lord it will be provided."
I call on the Lord in my distress, and he answers me. ~Psalm 120:1
Therefore encourage one another and build each other up, just as in fact you are doing. ~1 Thessalonians 5:11

Modern Names for Timeless Battles
2017 - 2018

Recycled book pages, hand carved, embellished with metallic pens. Reconstructed in original book cover, hand sewn with silk cord.

7.5 x 5.5 x 1.5 inches (folded)
7.5 x 70 inches (unfolded)

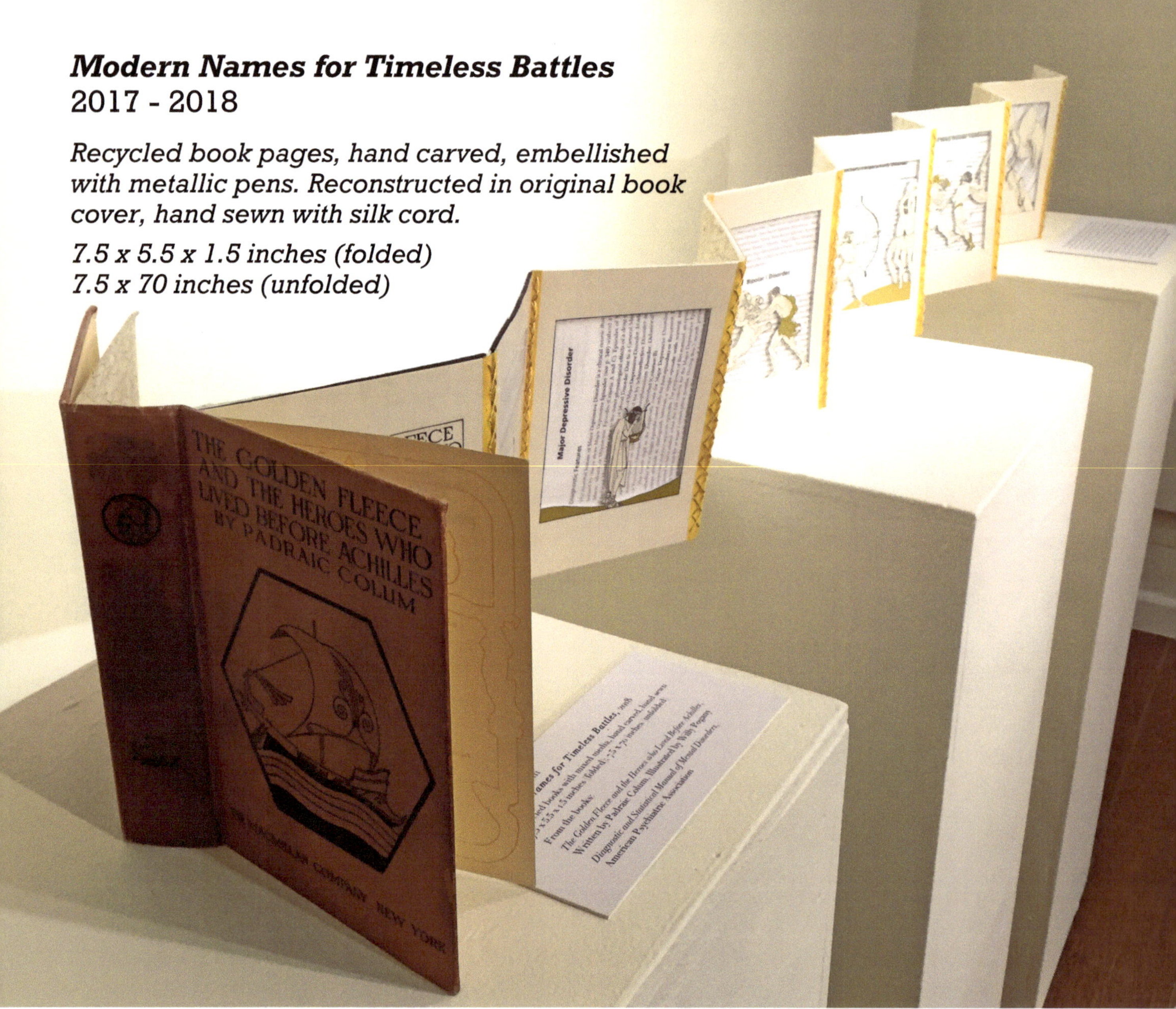

From the books, *The Golden Fleece and the Heroes Who Lived Before Achilles*, by Padraic Colum, illustrated by Willy Pogany; and the *Diagnostic and Statistical Manual of Mental Disorders*, by the American Psychiatric Association

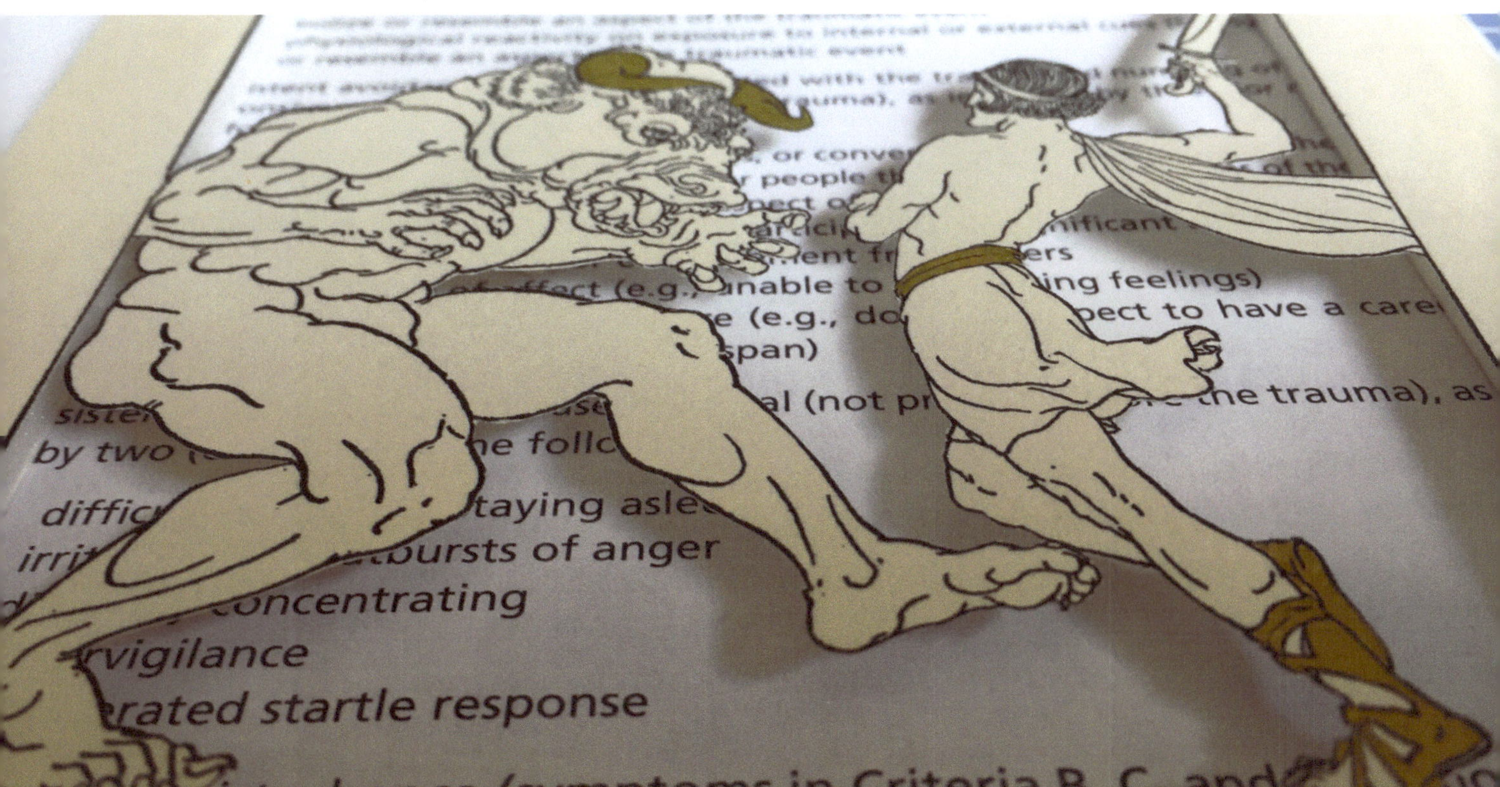

While flipping through a book I bought at a yard sale for a quarter, I suddenly found myself staring at an image that caught my breath. Gazing back at me was the embodiment of how PTSD *feels*. It's never easy to put into words, but somehow this one illustration of Theseus fighting the Minotaur captured everything I felt.

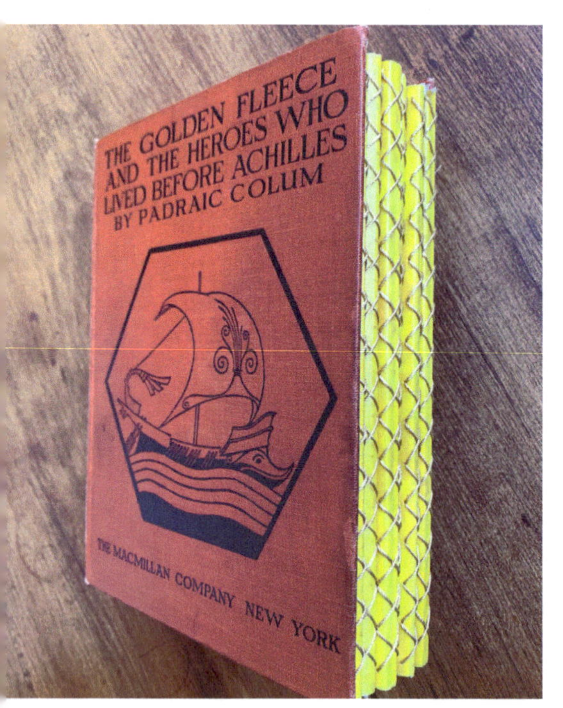
THE GOLDEN FLEECE
AND THE HEROES WHO
LIVED BEFORE ACHILLES
BY PADRAIC COLUM
THE MACMILLAN COMPANY NEW YORK

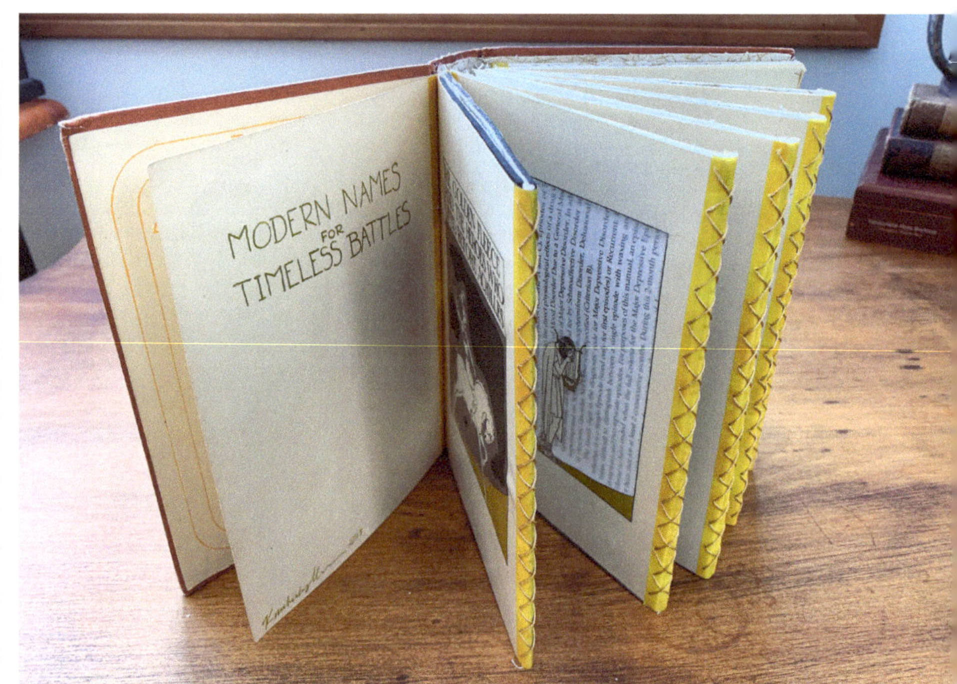
MODERN NAMES
FOR
TIMELESS BATTLES

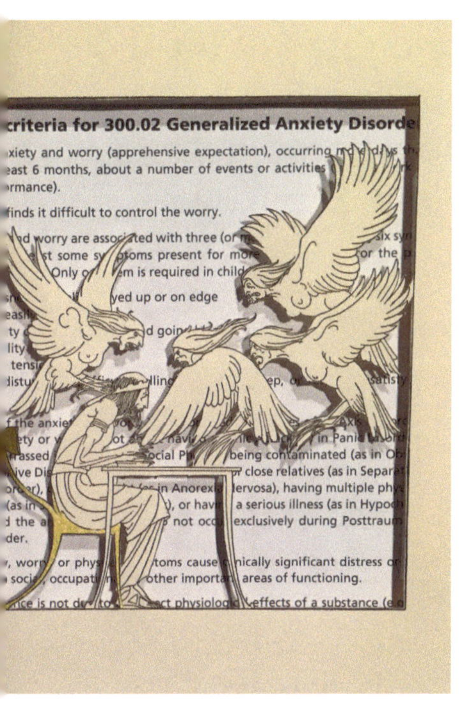

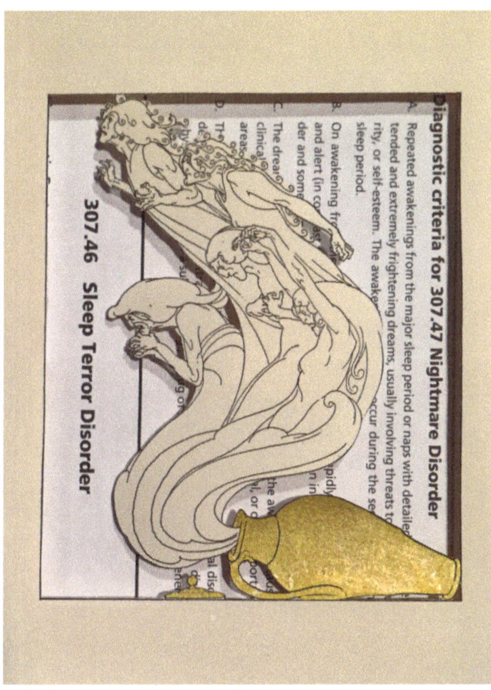

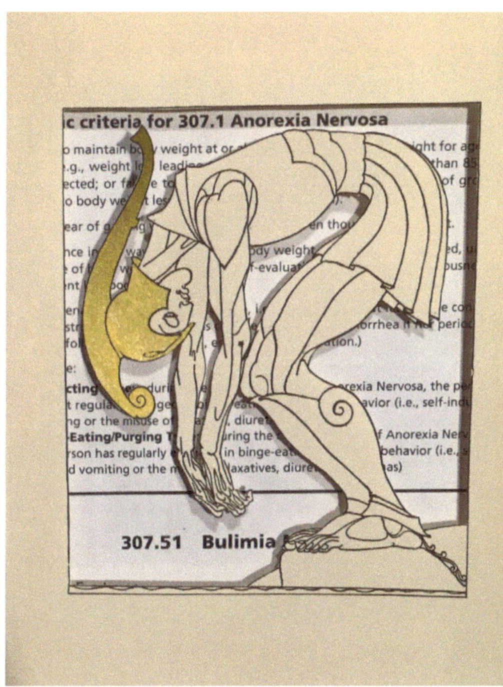

As I continued flipping through the book, other illustrations popped out at me, illustrations that embodied anxiety, nightmares, and other common struggles. It occurred to me, these struggles are shared throughout humanity—they're not confined to a specific place and time.

It doesn't matter much what we call these struggles. Post-Traumatic Stress Disorder didn't come into existence just because it was given a name after Vietnam. Before that, it was called "shellshock," and the same symptoms in women were considered "hysteria". Even in the past few years, in military circles at least, many people are dropping the "disorder" to simply call it "Post-Traumatic Stress." The same holds true for any other shared human experience: changing the name doesn't change the experience.

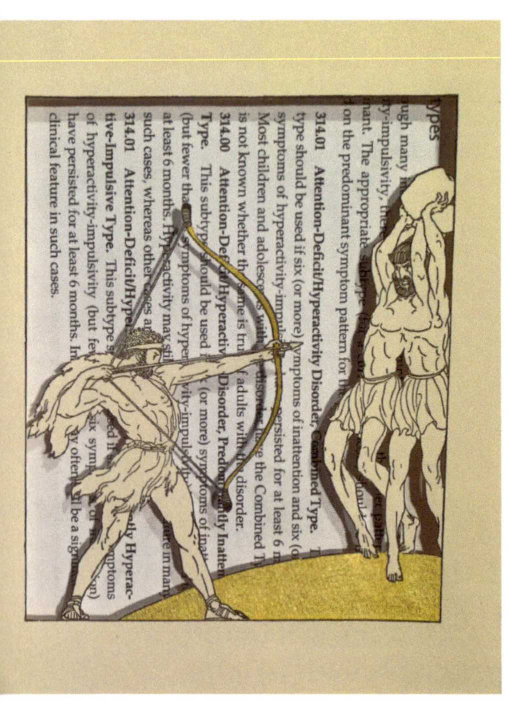

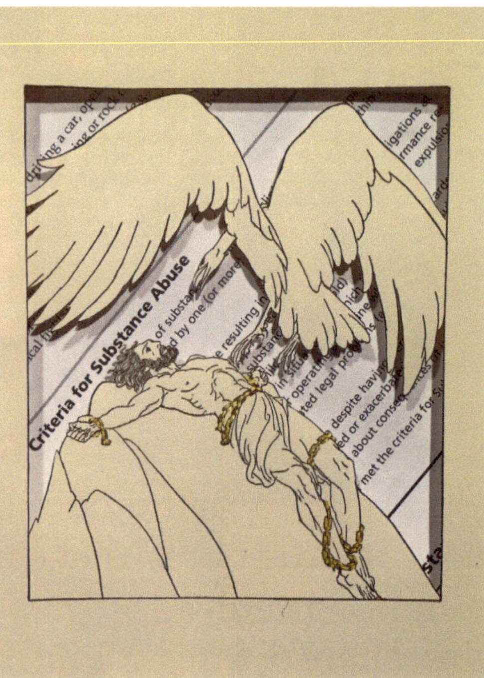

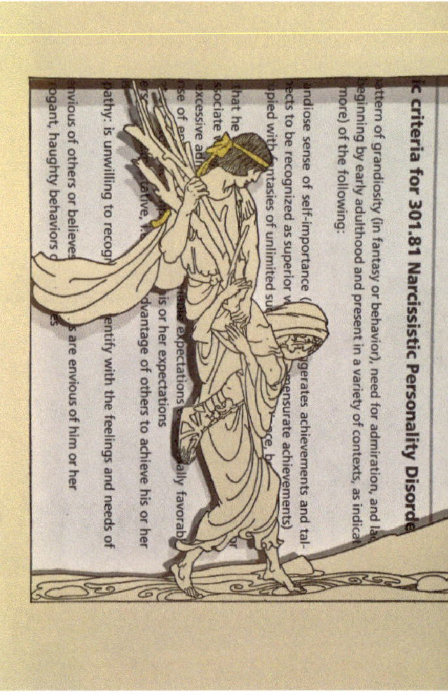

Since the beginning of time, humans have been battling.
We just keep renaming those battles.

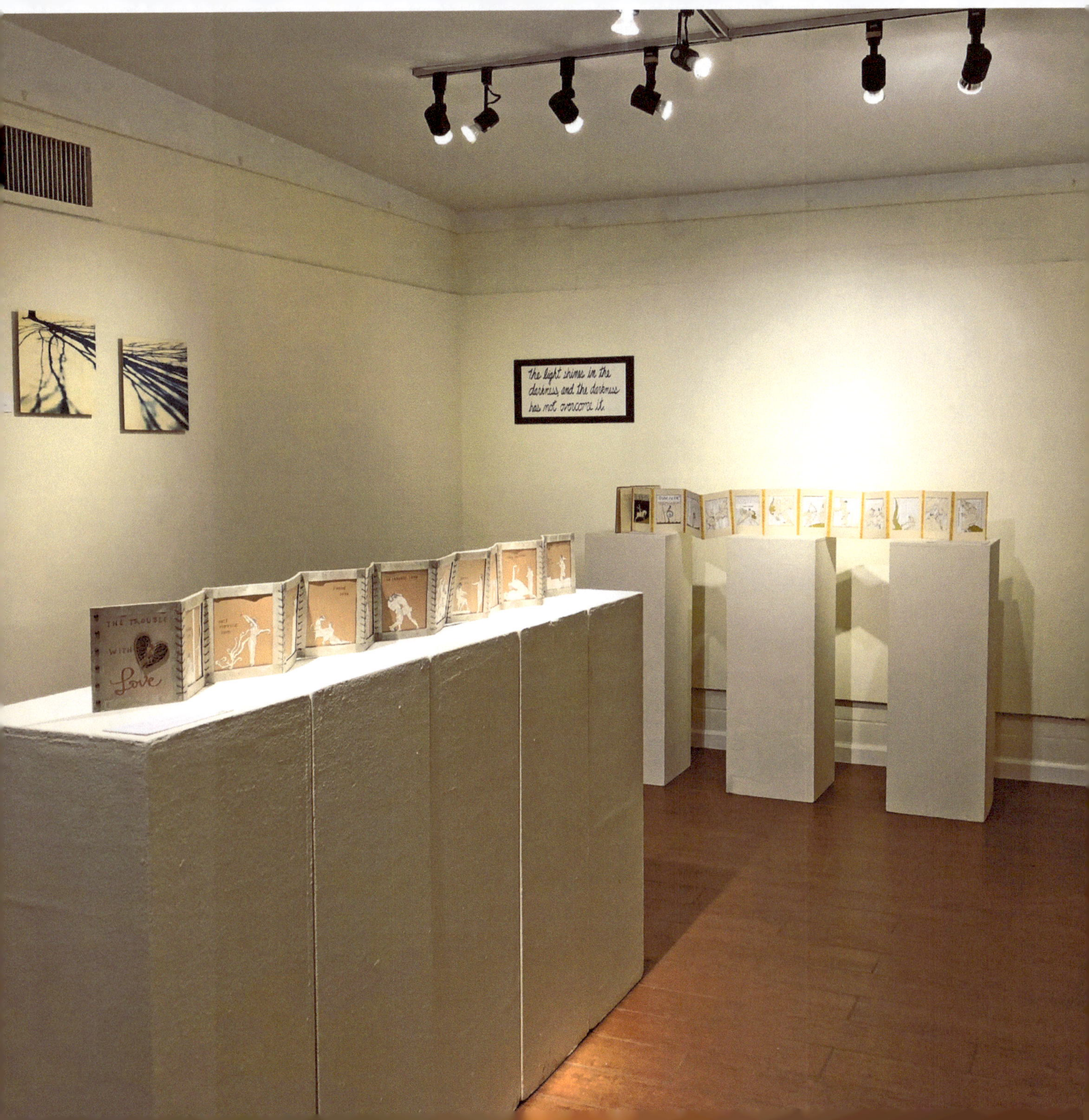
The light shines in the darkness, and the darkness has not overcome it.
THE TROUBLE WITH Love

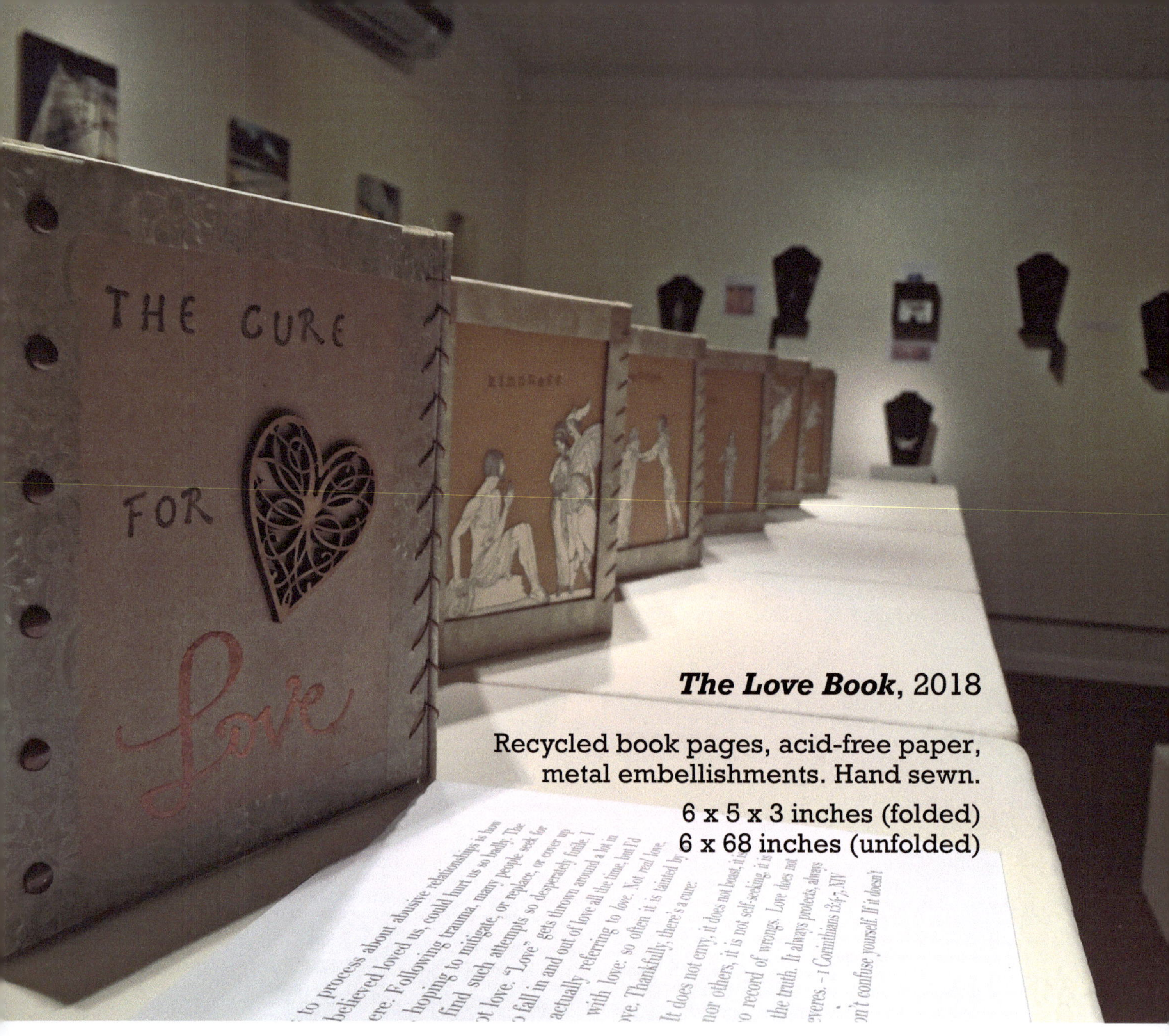

The Love Book, 2018

Recycled book pages, acid-free paper, metal embellishments. Hand sewn.

6 x 5 x 3 inches (folded)
6 x 68 inches (unfolded)

From the book, *The Golden Fleece and the Heroes Who Lived Before Achilles*, by Padraic Colum, illustrated by Willy Pogany

The Trouble with Love

One of the hardest things to process about abusive relationships is how someone we love, who we believed loved us, could hurt us so badly. The conundrum doesn't stop there. Following trauma, many people seek for love in all the wrong places, hoping to mitigate, or replace, or cover up their pain. It's frustrating to find such attempts so desperately futile.

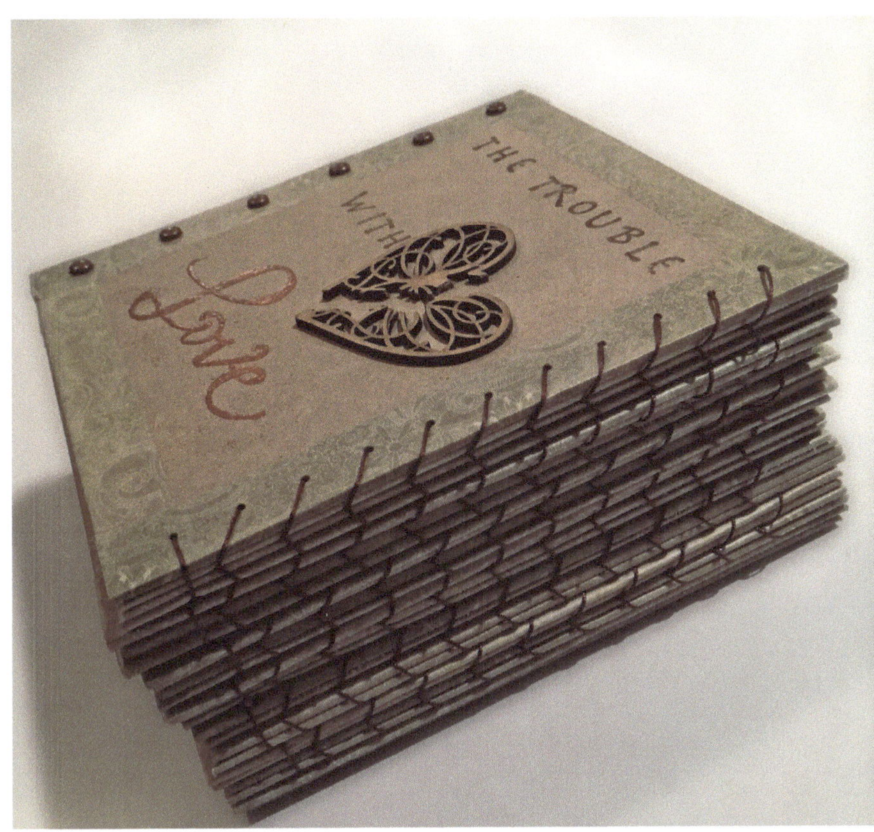

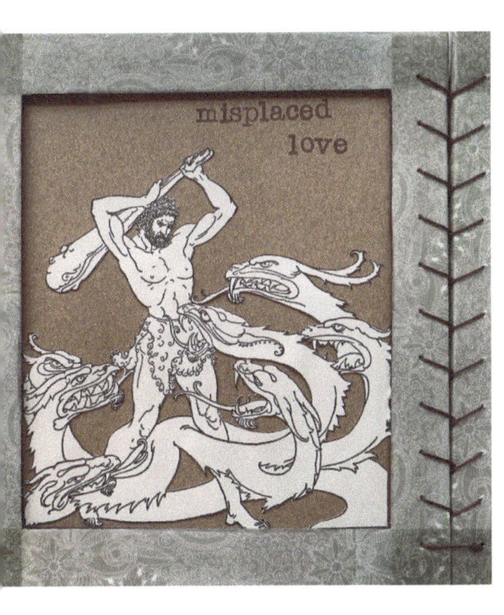

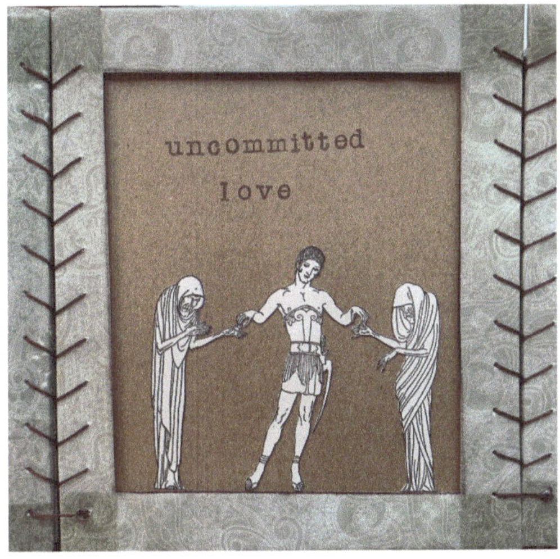

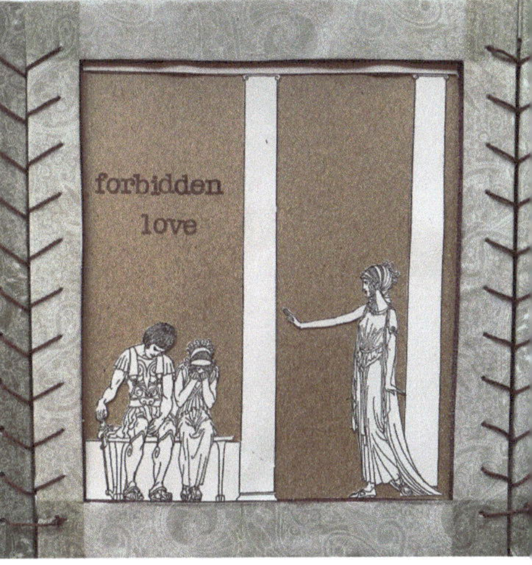

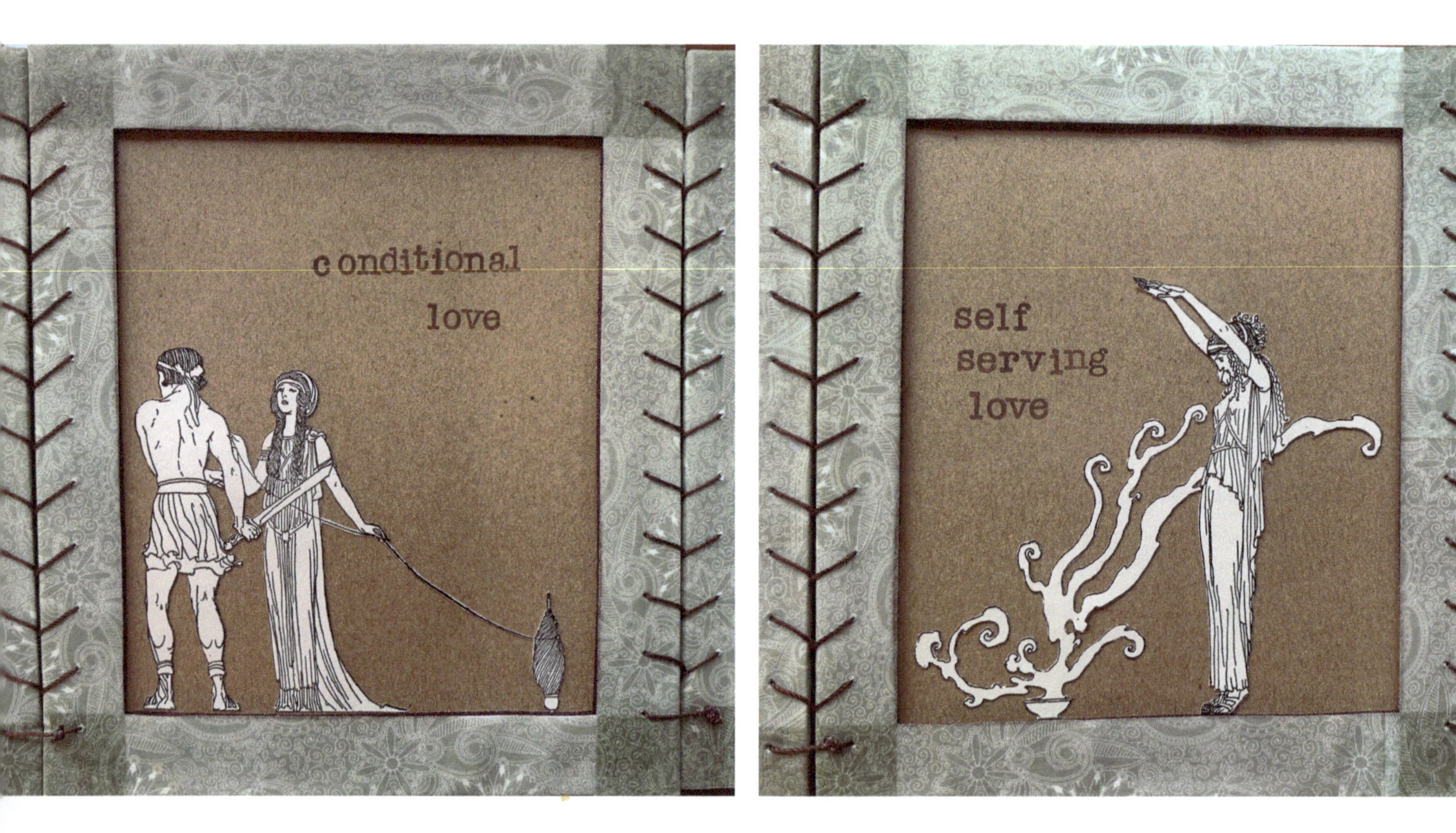

I realized, most of it's simply not love.

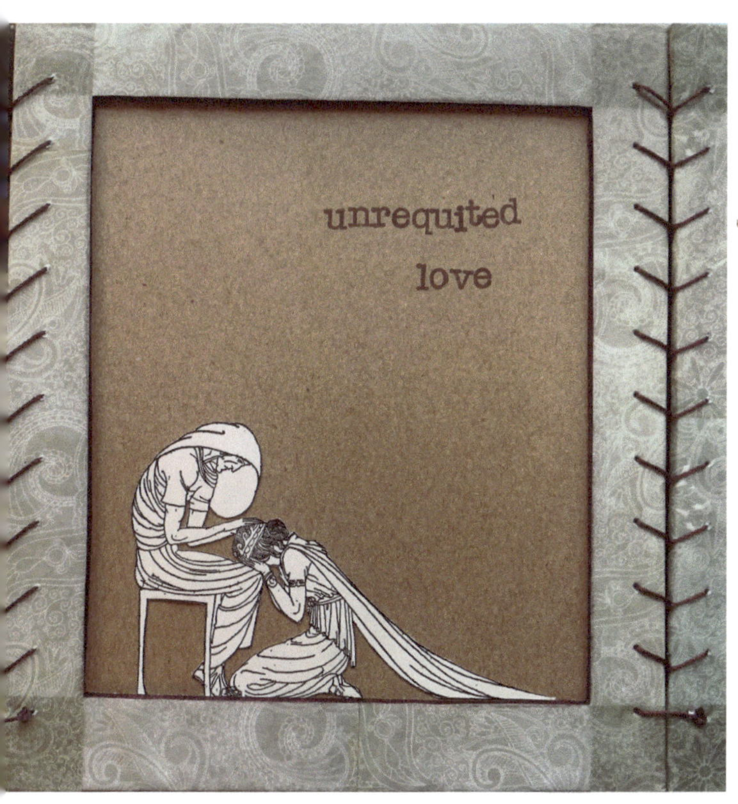

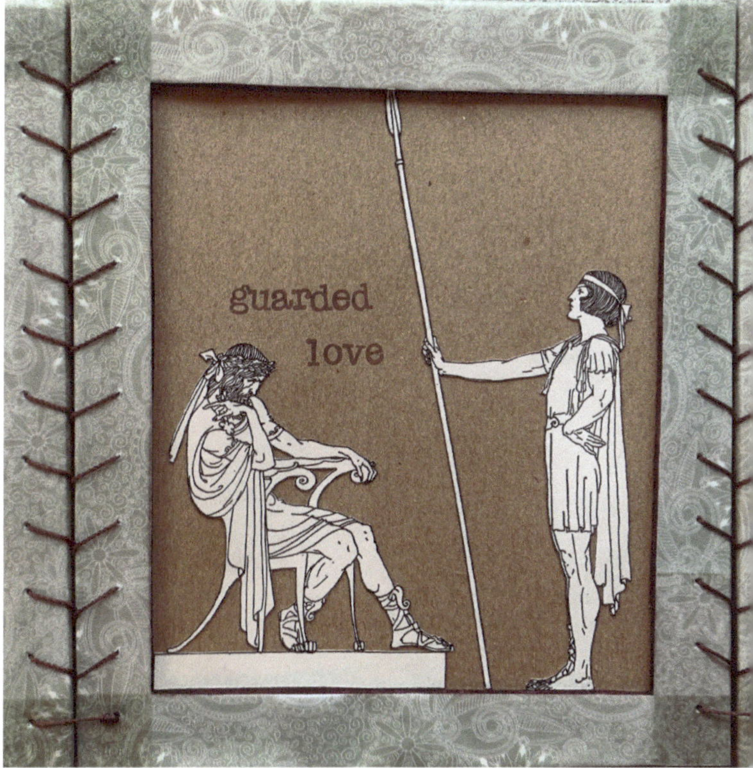

"Love" gets thrown around a lot in our culture. People claim to fall in and out of love all the time, but I'd argue that they're not usually actually referring to love. Not *real* love, anyway. And that's the trouble with love: so often it is tainted by, or confused with, things that aren't love.

Thankfully, there's a cure.

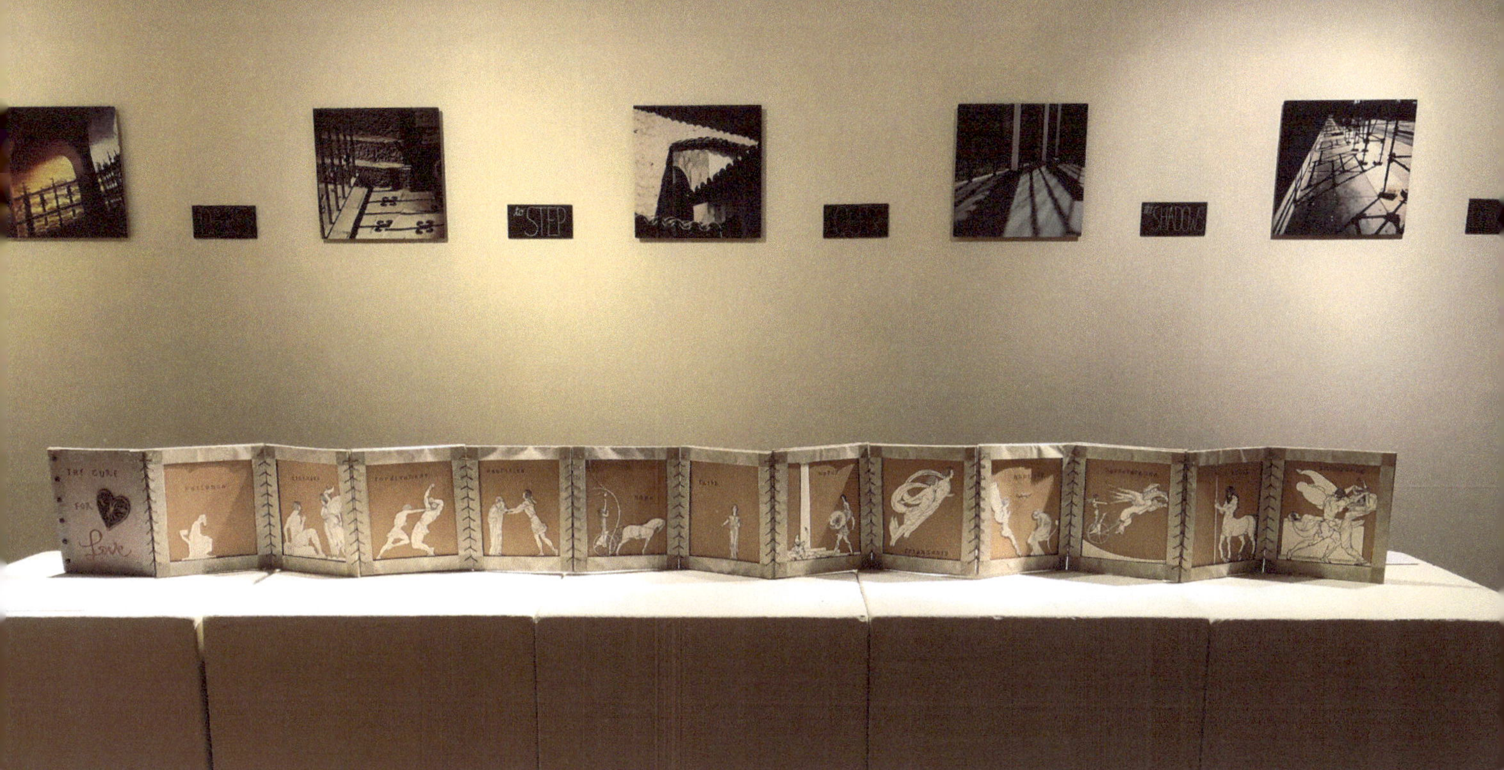

The Cure for Love

Love is patient, love is kind. It does not envy, it does not boast, it is not proud. It does not dishonor others, it is not self-seeking, it is not easily angered, it keeps no record of wrongs. Love does not delight in evil but rejoices with the truth. It always protects, always trusts, always hopes, always perseveres.

– 1 Corinthians 13:4-7, NIV

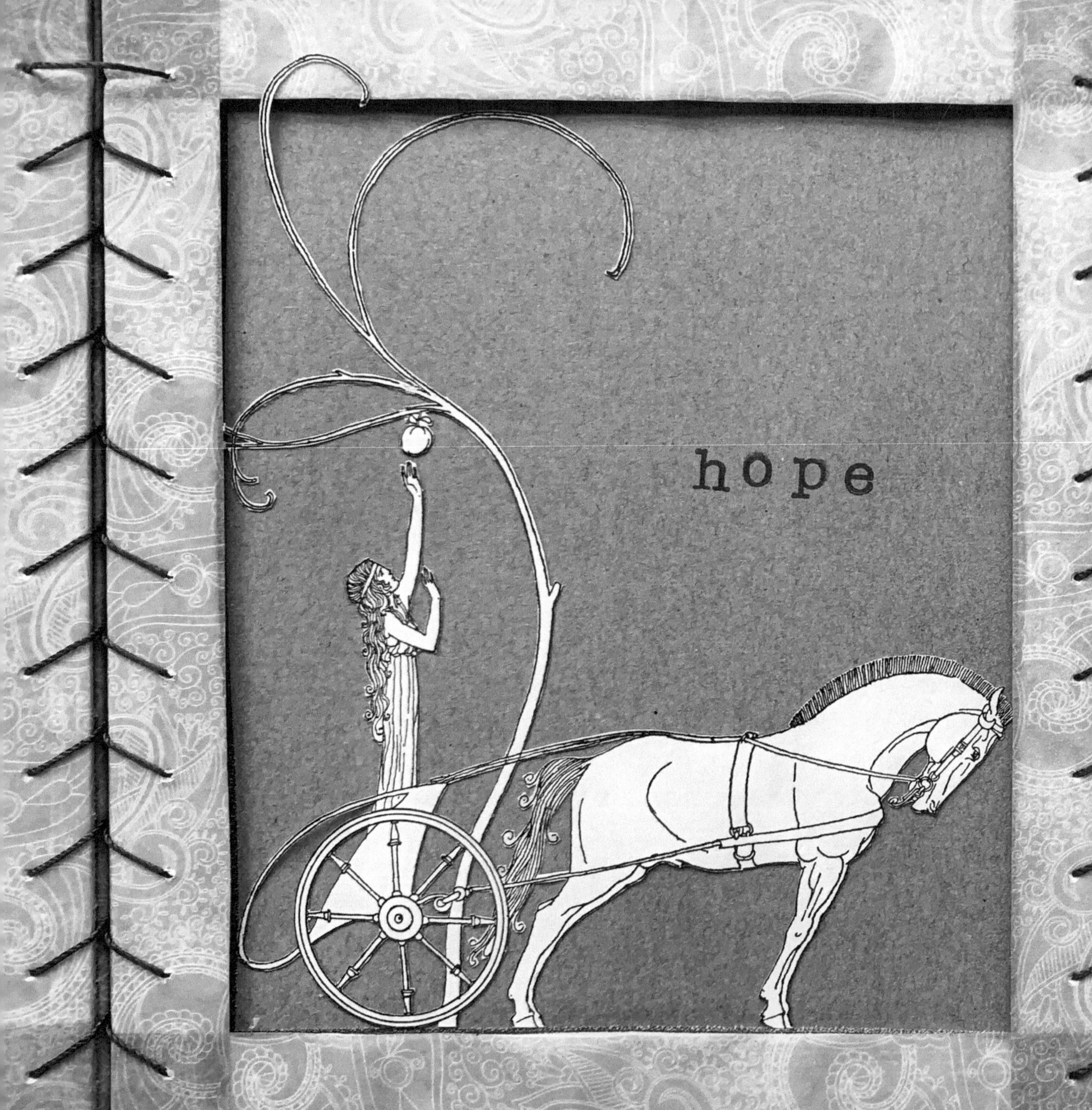

hope

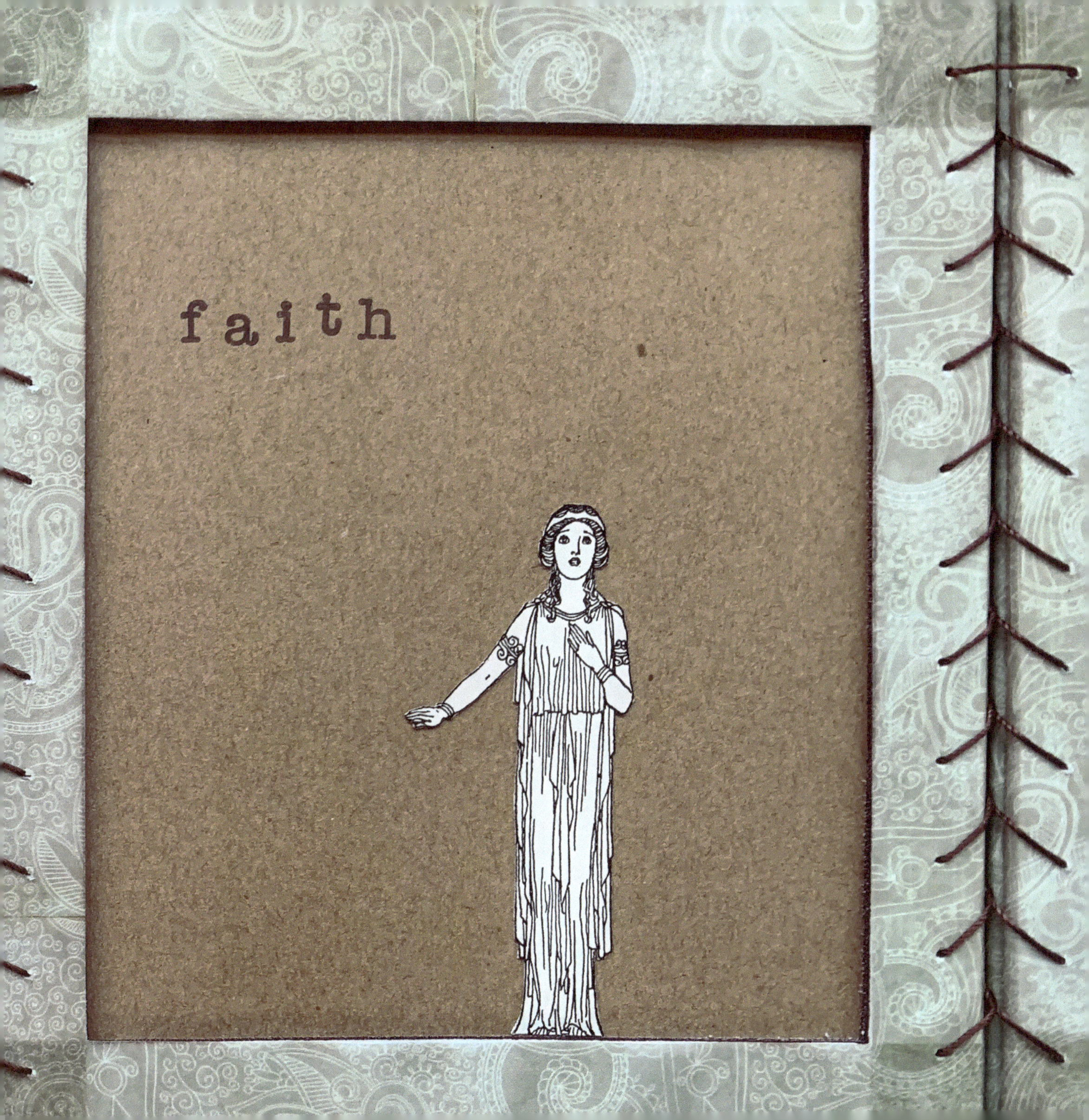
faith

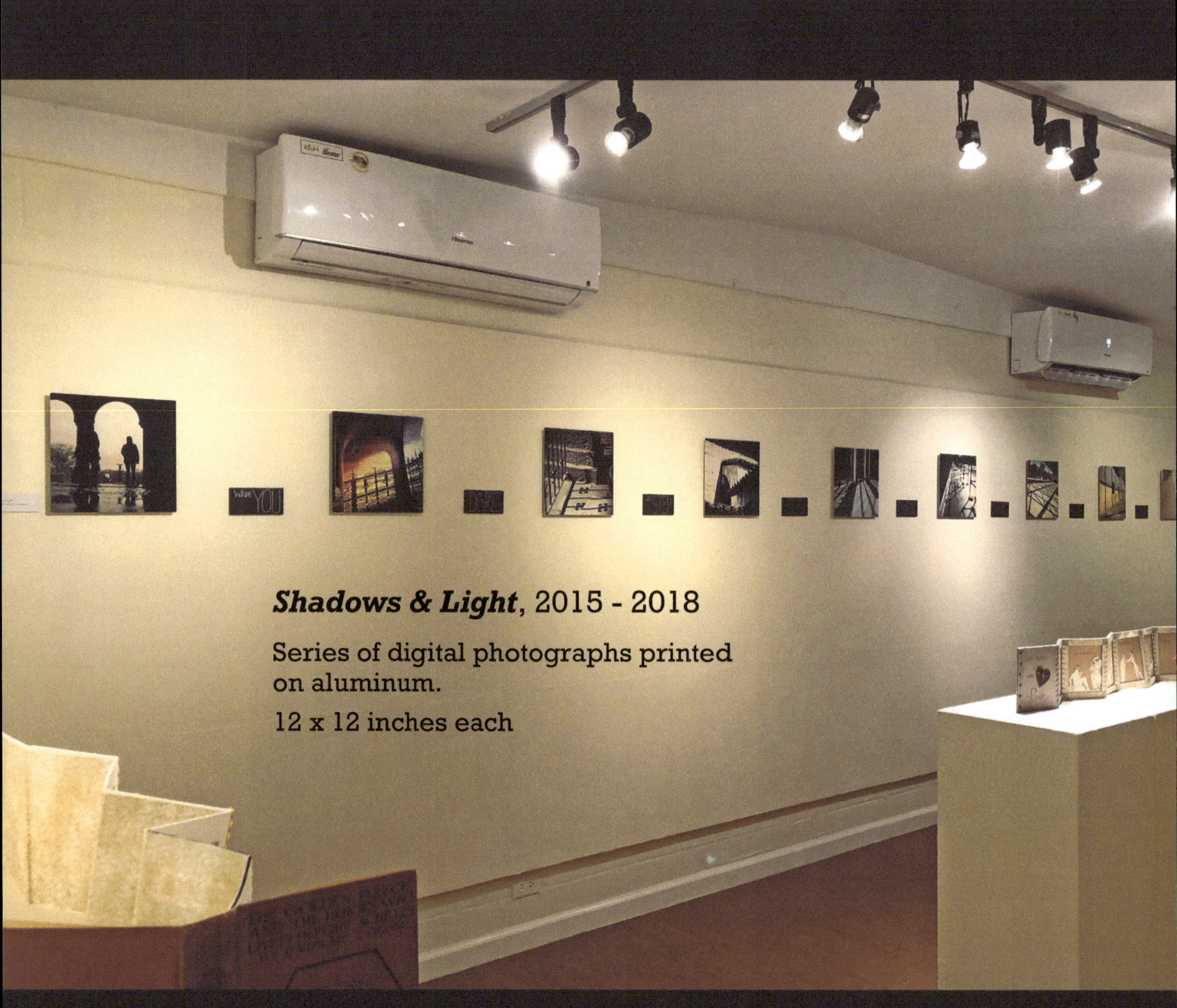

Shadows & Light, 2015 - 2018
Series of digital photographs printed on aluminum.
12 x 12 inches each

These photographs have been taken throughout this journey of learning to cope with PTSD. There's been an ongoing battle between darkness and light, but these photographs remind me that darkness doesn't have to remain simply that: dark and empty. There can be beauty in the shadows, as long as they don't overcome the light.

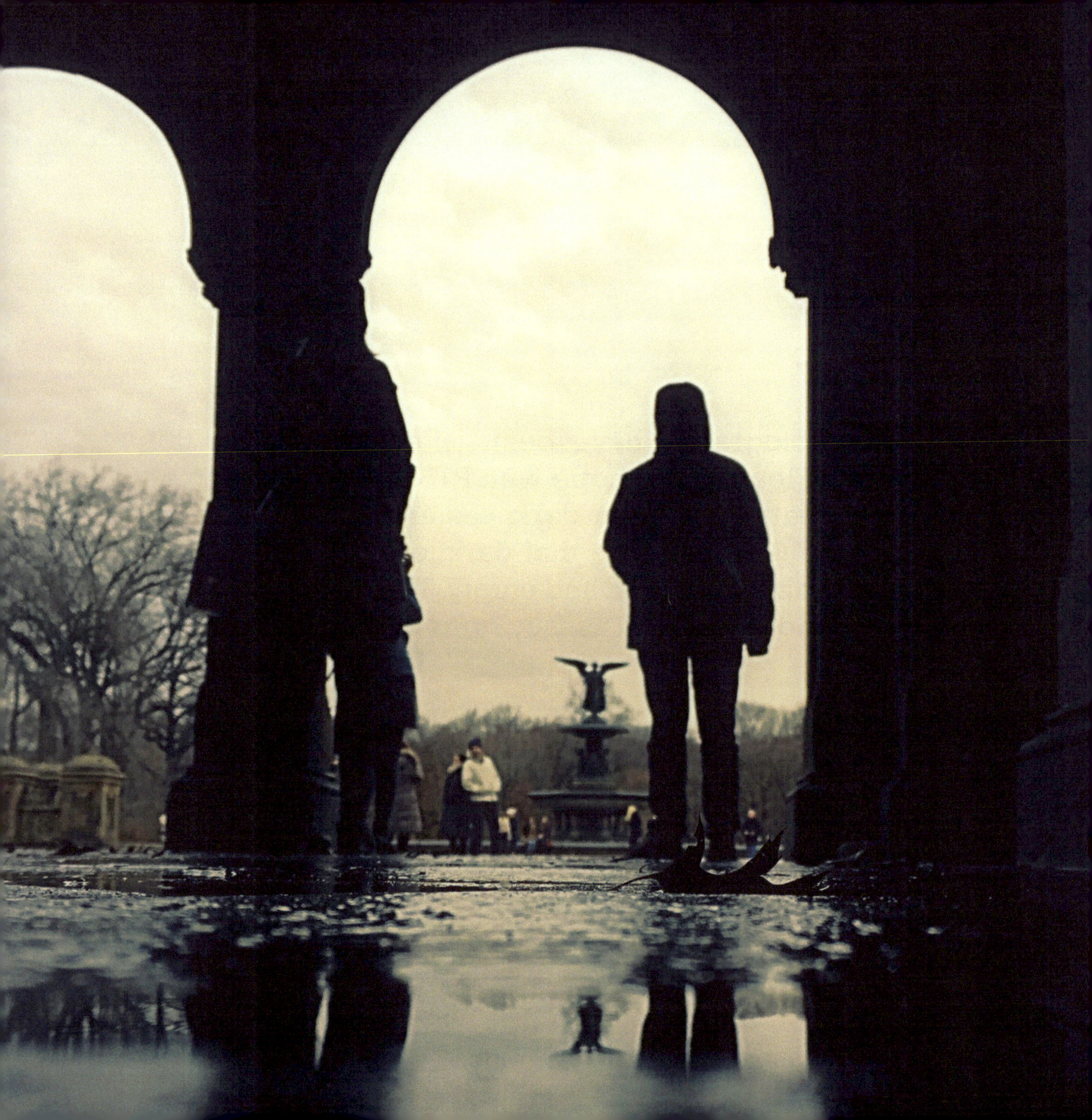

when you

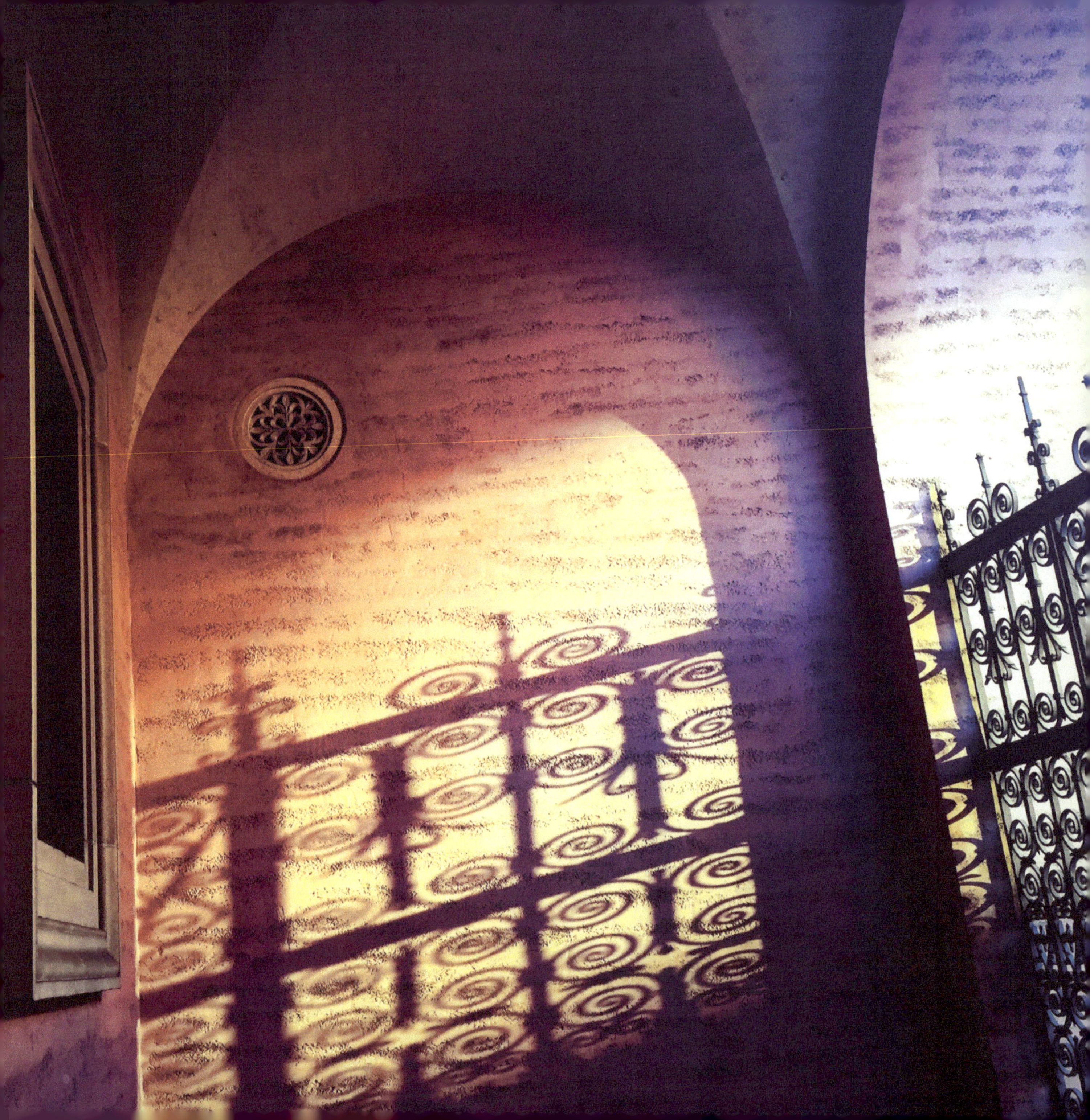

dare

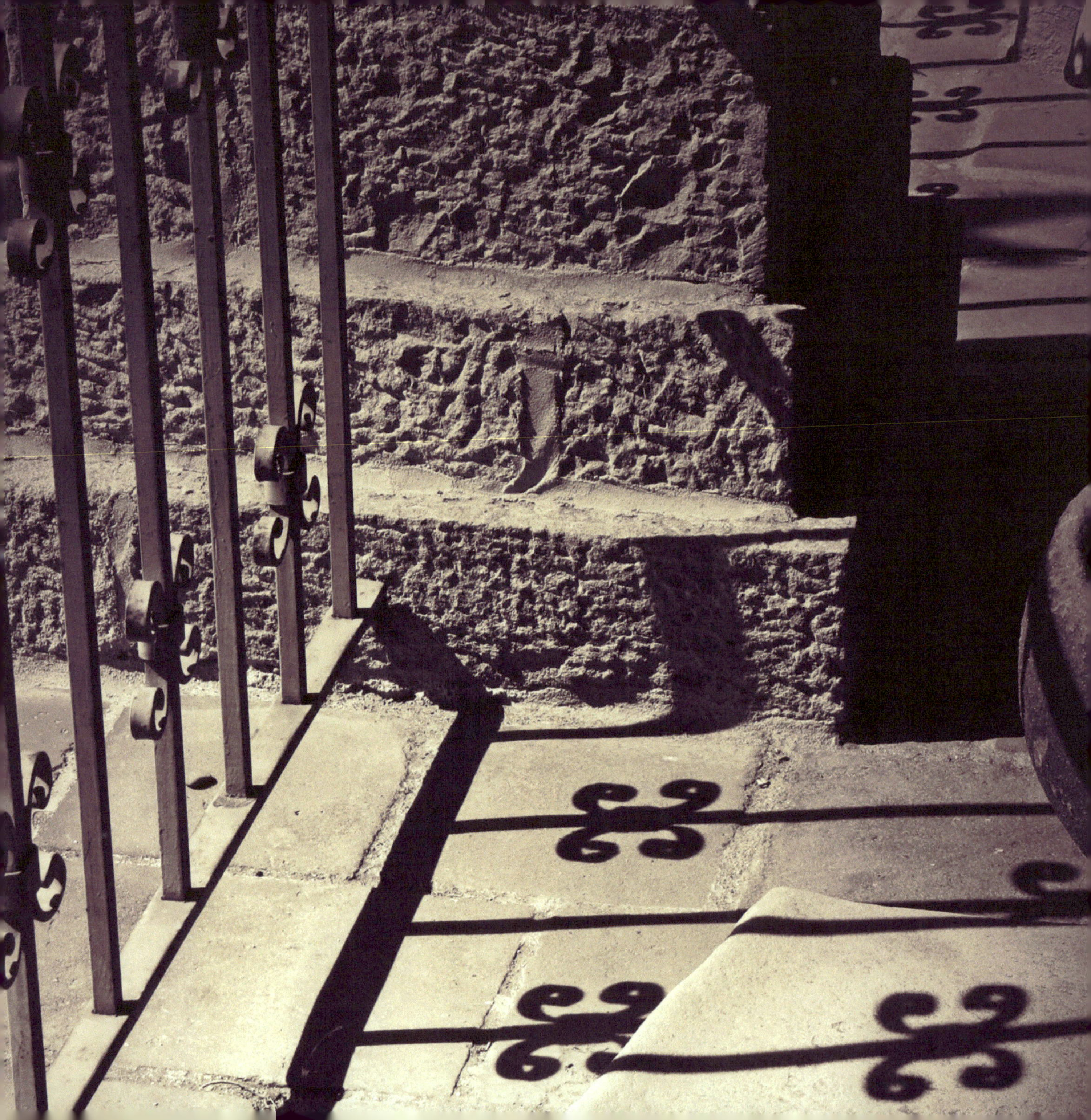

to step

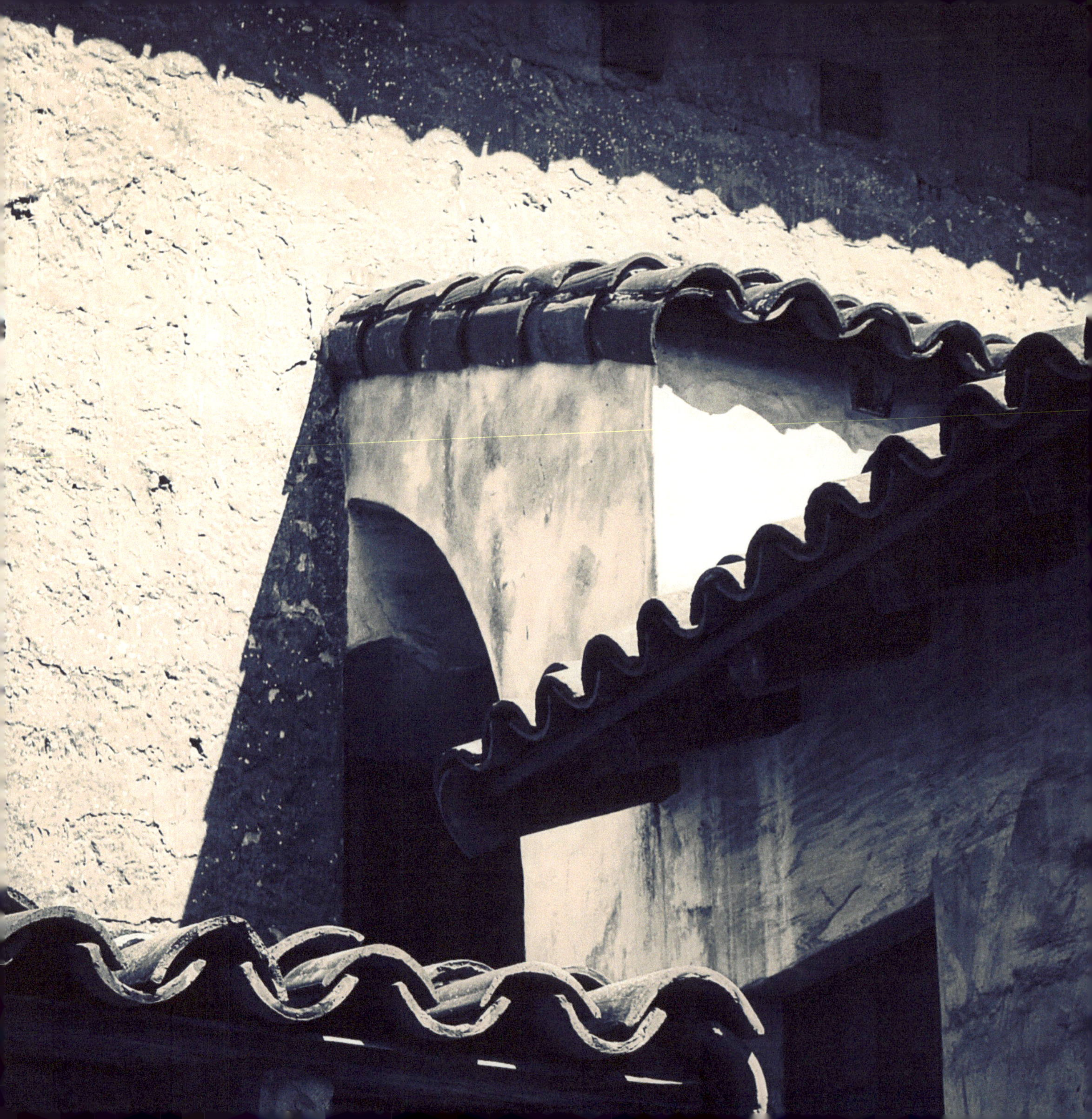

out of the shadows

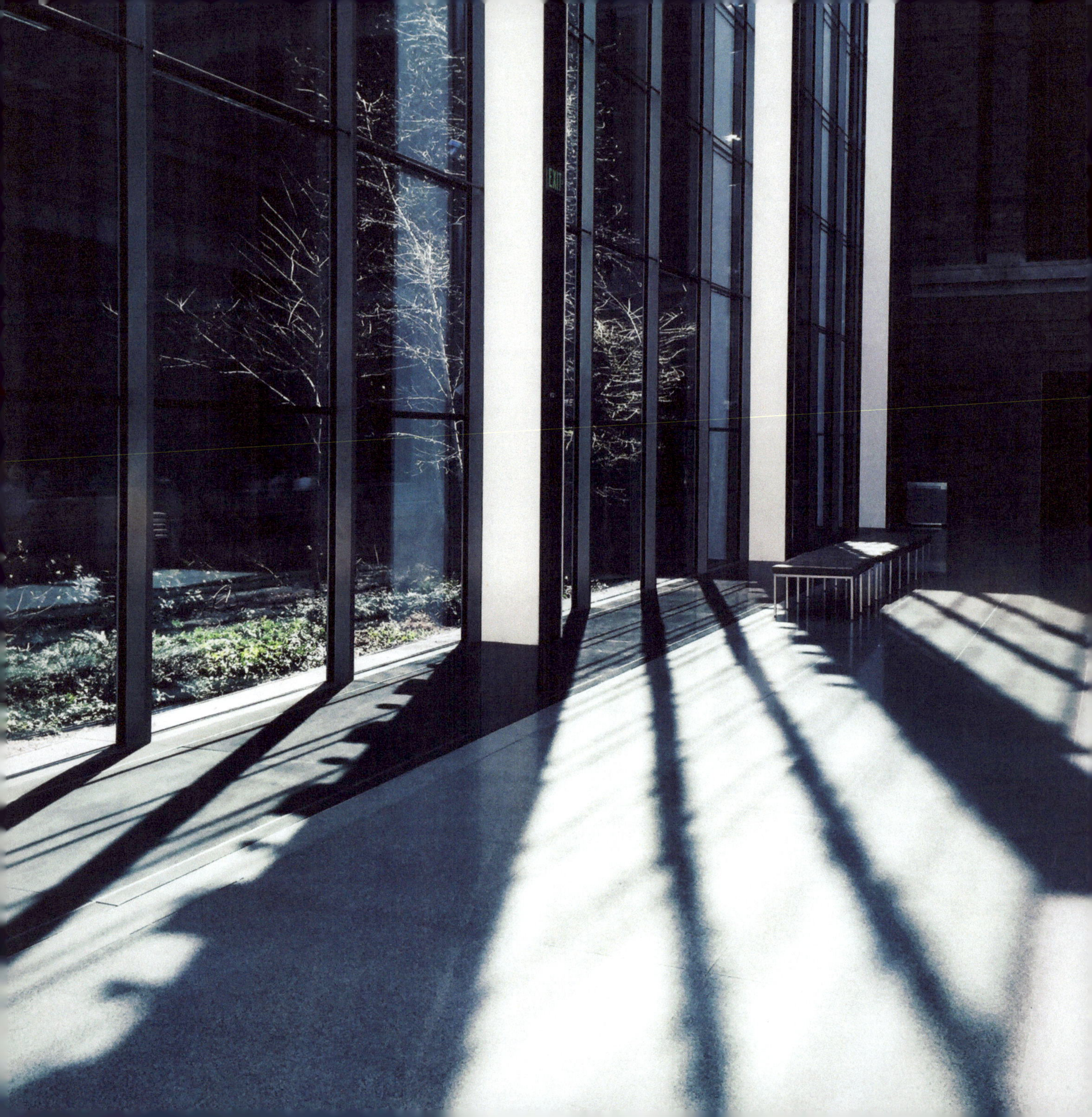

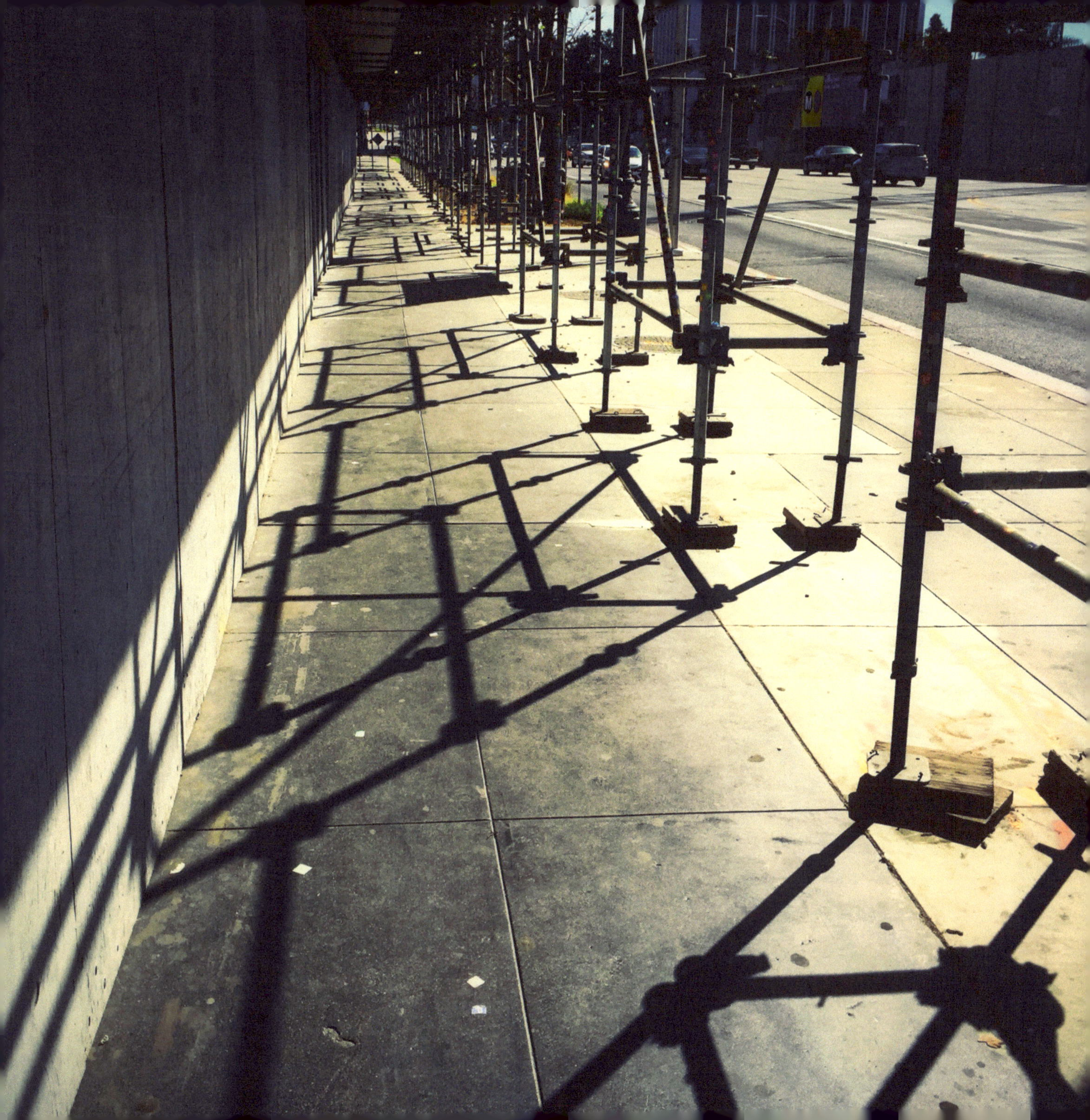

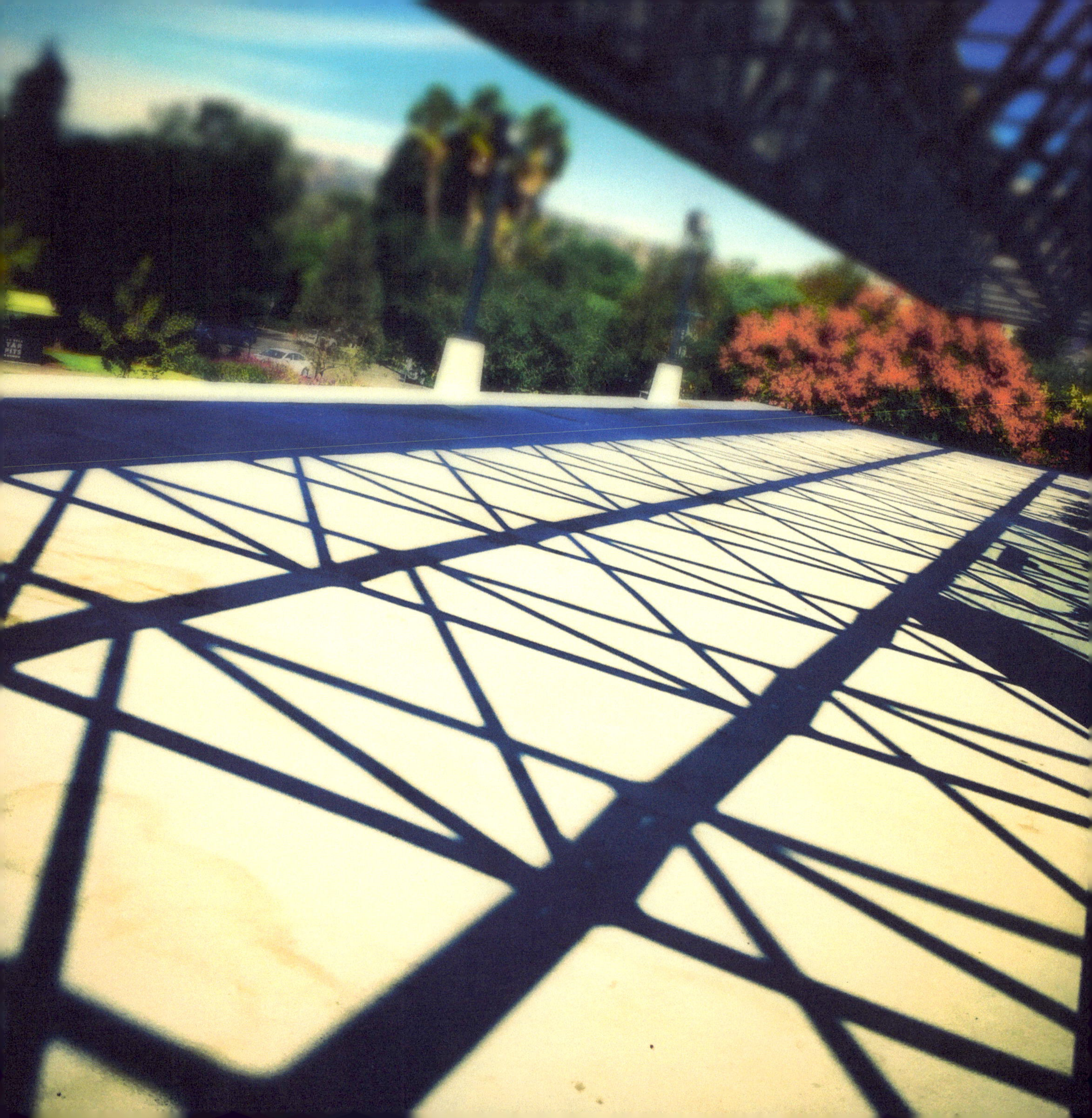

darkness

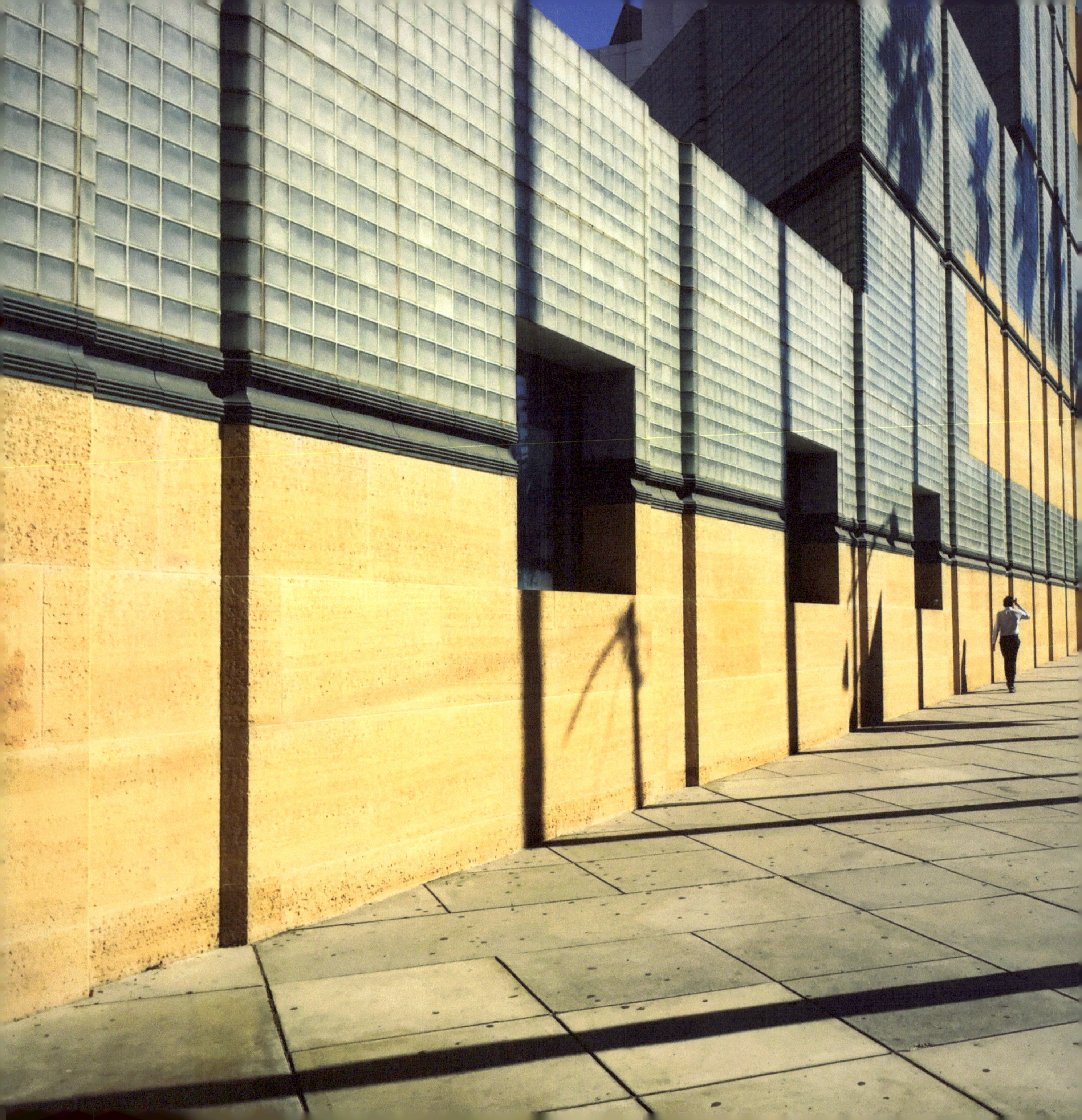

dissolves

into light

Acknowledgments

Thank you to the staff and faculty of the University of Guam, and Isla Center for the Arts. Special thanks to my mentor and advisor, Lewis Rifkowitz; and to Dr. Velma Yamashita, for her extensive help in the gallery before, during, and after the show.

Thank you to my parents for the love, support, and studio space that made it possible for me to create and heal. And to my brother, for encouraging me to finish what I started.

Thank you to my dear friends who were willing to travel across the globe with me to see my gallery. And to the many who have inspired me and cheered me on throughout the making of this book.

Thank you to my husband, Warren Lyon II, for your love, protection, and understanding. And for your mini masters in art installation.

All thanks to God Our Creator, who is a God of healing.

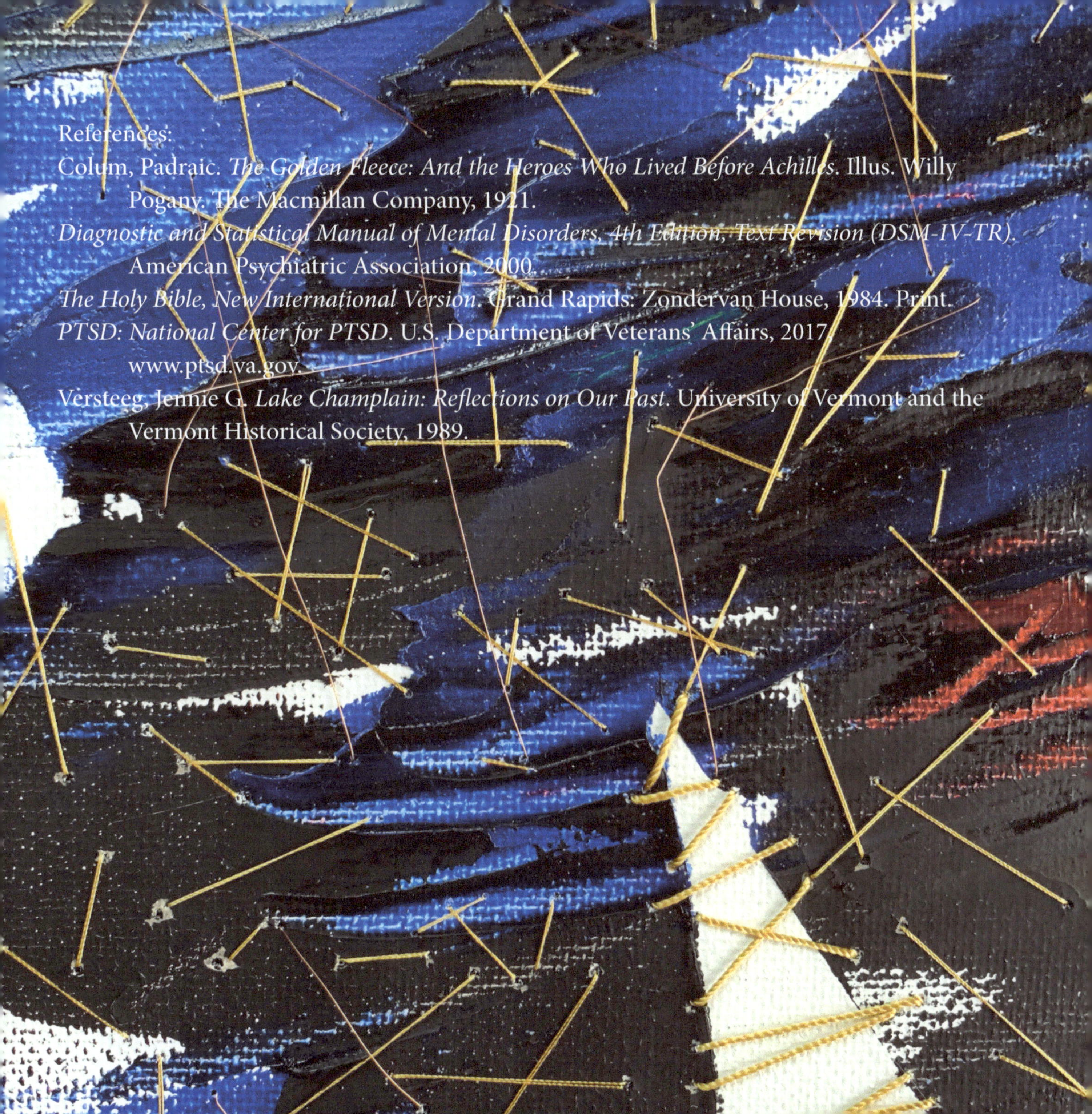

References:

Colum, Padraic. *The Golden Fleece: And the Heroes Who Lived Before Achilles*. Illus. Willy
    Pogany. The Macmillan Company, 1921.

Diagnostic and Statistical Manual of Mental Disorders, 4th Edition, Text Revision (DSM-IV-TR).
    American Psychiatric Association, 2000.

The Holy Bible, New International Version. Grand Rapids: Zondervan House, 1984. Print.

PTSD: National Center for PTSD. U.S. Department of Veterans' Affairs, 2017.
    www.ptsd.va.gov.

Versteeg, Jennie G. *Lake Champlain: Reflections on Our Past*. University of Vermont and the
    Vermont Historical Society, 1989.